The Wealth Weapon

The authors are _hard right_ conservatives !!

The Wealth Weapon

U.S. Foreign Policy and Multinational Corporations

Ben J. Wattenberg
Richard J. Whalen

Transaction Books
New Brunswick (U.S.A.) and London (U.K.)

Library of Congress Catalog Number: 79-66448
ISBN: 0-87855-340-1 (cloth), 0-87855-820-9 (paper)
Printed in the United States of America

Library of Congress Cataloging in Publication Data
Wattenberg, Ben J
  The wealth weapon.

  Includes index.
  1. Corporations, American.   2. International business enterprises.   3. United States—Foreign economic relations.
I. Whalen, Richard J., 1935-   joint author.
II. Title.
HD2795.W3   338.8′8   79-66448
ISBN 0-87855-340-1
ISBN 0-87855-820-9 pbk.

Contents

Chapter   Page

1. The Wealth Weapon: An Introduction   1

2. The Issue Is Stated:
   Wealth-Making and World-Shaping   5

3. A Businessman   16

4. A Labor Leader   40

5. A Foreign Policy Activist   53

6. A Third World Leader   76

7. Rebuttals   83

8. Who's Right, Who's Wrong?   107

Index   123

1.

The Wealth Weapon: An Introduction

This slender volume has a curious history. It began as a book about a small, if fascinating, cranny of economic policy. It was to be a book about multinational corporations (MNCs). It ended up as that—but also as a personal testament about geopolitics dealing with the dangerous global circumstances of America today. In that context it presents a suggested partial remedy, which we call "the wealth weapon."

It is also a curious book in that it predicts a course of action that in some small part came to pass before the book was published. As our ideas developed, we came to see a global power puzzle that seemed to demand a new response by the United States—an economic response. And so, as will be seen in these pages, a case is made that the U.S. government ought to pull its socks up and take a broad look at just what tools, levers, scalpels, carrots and sticks it has available to wage a foreign policy in a time when military power balances in the world may have tipped against us.

We were writing such ideas in this manuscript in 1976 and 1977. Now, cosmic thinkers may come to similar conclusions; that is a fact known to a small army of scientists who claim that *they* should have won the Nobel Prize, not the man who actually received it.

And so, in 1978, it was learned that a task force of the National

Security Council (NSC), chaired by Dr. Samuel Huntington, had quietly engaged itself in exactly such a far-flung review. Then, in the summer of 1978, when the Kremlin cracked down on Soviet dissidents, when American patience was worn thin over Soviet adventurism in Africa, the fruits of the NSC review were available for sampling. Could America send the Soviets a message of displeasure that went beyond rhetoric and yet remain safely short of a shot across the bow? After much "to-ing" and "fro-ing" the Carter administration ultimately decided that a computer, previously licensed, would not be sold to the Soviets. A small matter, to be sure. Probably more important, it was decreed that American oil drilling equipment was, for the first time since the 1950s, shifted to a "controlled" list that could be approved or disapproved on the basis of national security considerations. A small matter again? Maybe not. Oil could be the economic jugular of the Soviet Union.

While these actions fell well short of a bolder course of action urged by Senator Henry Jackson, among others, they were not idle gestures. These actions, we believe, should have signaled the beginning of a new, or at least modified, world strategy for the United States. In our terms, although not the president's, it resembled nothing less than the first tentative presidential unsheathing of the wealth weapon.

It could be argued (by a fool) that such events might eliminate the need for this volume. Not so. As we hope readers will discover, the idea of the wealth weapon is a potent one only when it represents a coherent understanding of the world situation and a firm resolve to act with purposeful vigor on the world stage. At this moment, despite the economic studies initiated by the Carter administration, it is not at all clear whether the action officers of American foreign policy have such an understanding or such resolve. Some do. And many, too many, don't. A few months after all the talk about "trade as a weapon" within the Carter administration, two cabinet officers (Blumenthal and Kreps) were in Moscow with 300 American businessmen lobbying on the side of the Russians to relax U.S. trade restrictions with no reciprocity requested! And so we feel this volume is more necessary than ever.

This volume is also curious from another point of view. It is in the form of a dialogue—actually a quadralogue. There is a reason for this: as we began exploring on our own the tangled trail of economic policy formulation, a path that leads from multinational corporations on to trade policy and ultimately to the wealth weapon, we realized that there were no simple sets of facts that could be presented to the readers as definitive.

After all, it took us three years of on-and-off labor to put together this volume. We visited seventeen nations on four continents, interviewed more than a hundred persons, pored over mind-numbing charts and tables and data that seem to do nothing more than pile fresh abstractions upon earlier abstractions.

We talked to Japanese union officials, Brazilian generals and Brazilian antigovernment intellectuals, Swiss bankers, German industrialists, British Cabinet ministers, Russian officials and scholars, Taiwanese clothing manufacturers, toy assemblers in Hong Kong, Chinese trade officials, Iranian businessmen and so many, many Americans—for this is essentially a book about an American situation. We talked to Americans in America—union officials, multinational businessmen, bankers, politicians, economists, scholars, foreign policy experts and assorted appointed cabinet and subcabinet level officials from both Republican and Democratic administrations. And we talked to other Americans outside of America: a bridge-builder, a bubble gum manufacturer, tire makers, bankers, consulting engineers, mining entrepreneurs, members of the AFL-CIO on international duty and some patient and helpful U.S. embassy officials.

And when we finished we realized that neither of us had ever dealt with a more complicated and arcane subject, or a more important one.

But there weren't simple facts. The computers, it's true, spew out numbers, but contending sides choose to use different numbers and challenge the numbers used by others.

Facts may be hard to come by, but arguments proliferate. And because the subject is at least as much political as economic, arguments may end up having more weight than facts. This, then, is a book about arguments. For most effective presentation, arguments demand protagonists.

We present here four fictional composite characters and one real one. The fictional characters represent some of the major parties involved in the heated debate about multinationals and about economic policy. "A Businessman" sets forth the views from inside the corporate world; "A Labor Leader" also presents an inside view, but from a very different perspective. A bitter man called "A Third World Leader" brings in a foreign dimension. The fourth character, "A Foreign Policy Activist," also deals with international applications, but from a particular American point of view.

The four characters represent composite distillations of the hundreds of persons we have interviewed and thousands of pages we have read.

The fifth composite character is, of course, us. As authors, needless to say, we wholly control the strings that make our characters jump. Furthermore, a good deal, but not all, of what the "Foreign Policy Activist" says represents our views. Finally, at the end of the book, we walk on stage to speak briefly in our own voice.

But a funny thing happened on the way to the end. As in real fiction (as opposed to this fake fiction), the characters took on a life of their own. Having established their general intellectual position early on in this volume, they then turned out to wage fiery rhetorical combat almost as if their masters, we the authors, did not exist. Accordingly, we think that the combat described here is authentic. We have also come to the conclusion that it is very important combat indeed—for the argument described here may well play an important role in shaping the nature of the world we will live in.

Enough talk then. It's a curious and unconventional book, believe us. After a few moments to describe some history, we give these pages to four angry men, and offer to the reader a keyhole for eavesdropping.

2.

The Issue Is Stated:
Wealth-Making and World-Shaping

Significantly, in all of the mountains of literature produced about multinational corporations, no expert has yet produced a working definition that most other experts are prepared to accept. Thus, the arguments begin at the very beginning.

How many countries does a big corporation have to do business in to qualify as "multinational"? Two? Twenty? Can a multinational corporation be modest-sized or must it be big? Precisely how big does a corporation have to be to be big? A quarter of a billion dollars in sales? Half a billion? A billion? Five billion?

Are all "multinationals" a problem? Does a copper mining corporation that goes where the copper is raise the same problems as a "runaway" dress manufacturer which employs twelve-year-old Asian girls who work sewing machines sixty hours a week in unsafe factories? Is a $30 billion oil company analogous to anything else? Can it now be analogous to anything else if it must deal with a foreign government-controlled producer cartel?

What about a sophisticated manufacturing company that sets up overseas plants to produce goods based on American licenses, but does so in some measure because foreign officials have told the company that its goods would be kept out by tariffs unless some jobs and plants were located in the consuming nation?

And what about banks that move tens of billions of dollars of investment capital from nation to nation? Aren't they an entirely different matter?

No matter. The Great Phrase-Maker has been at work again. Having run through "immoral war," "re-order priorities" and "trauma of Watergate" the G.P.M. has given us a new catch-all to conjure with: "multinational corporation." And so, "the multinational corporation," whatever it means, has become a major "issue" all over the world. In the halls of Congress, in the corridors of the United Nations, in clamorous assemblies of those hundred-or-so nations of the "Third World," in the plush boardrooms of giant corporations, in courtrooms where criminal cases are being heard and in the White House, the same phrase, with overtones of mystery, power and conspiracy, rings forth: "multinational corporation." Why?

For generations, American business has been international in scope. As early as the 1870s, Singer Sewing Machine Company had successful production facilities in Scotland and was selling half its total output overseas. Nevertheless, the phrase "multinational corporation," and the set of problems and controversies that it has come to represent, has emerged only in recent years. It has become an issue, a problem and a controversy in large measure because of an almost uncanny confluence of events and conditions that are, surprisingly, mostly unrelated to each other. But their coming together has merged a series of discrete, smaller problems and created a single major issue.

It may be useful to begin by listing some of those conditions and events that have flowed together in recent years to form the backdrop of the multinational problem. A number of distinct elements are evident.

The Perception of Job Export

There are few American-made transistor radios. New England shoe towns have become ghost towns. Television sets for American homes are manufactured in Japan. Clothing factories have moved from New England to South Carolina, and then to Hong Kong. And the number of imported passenger cars climbed from 57,000 in 1955 to 449,000 in 1960 to 2,237,075 in 1978. And in each instance, Americans lost their jobs, or did not gain potential jobs.

The phenomenon, of course, is not a new one. Factories open and close. Whole industries flourish and disappear. Mining towns spring up and decline. Workers employed at skilled and responsible jobs are suddenly unemployed.

Such is the harsh logic of capitalism. Adam Smith called it the doctrine of "comparative advantage." Simply stated, Smith described a process where society as a whole benefits when "the most efficient producer" is allowed to sell his goods anywhere, with as few artificial barriers (such as tariffs) as possible. It is a process that has worked well since Smith published *The Wealth of Nations* in 1776.

If cameras can be made better and/or less expensively in Japan than in Illinois, if shoes can be produced more efficiently and elegantly in Rome, Italy than Rome, New York, if Japanese and Germans can design and make better small cars than Americans—so be it. That's what "free trade" is supposed to determine. After all, with their Yankee dollars, those Japanese, Germans and Italians supposedly will turn around and buy Yankee computers, Yankee airplanes and grain from the Midwest—items that *we* can produce better and more efficiently than *they*. Theoretically, according to the advocates of free trade, the man who lost his job in a shoe plant in Haverhill, Massachusetts soon will get another job, likely a better one, at a Route 128 electronics factory producing the semiconductors that go into American-made computers.

Well and good. But in recent years, in America, several factors have interfered with this neat, logical view of the nature of economic enterprise and the wealth of nations.

For the United States the years following World War II were uniquely secure and bountiful in several ways. When the guns fell silent in 1945 the United States was the only major economy intact and functioning in the world. To her credit, the United States directly and indirectly gave massive assistance to revitalize both former friends and foes. The Marshall Plan and Point Four provided direct assistance to the devastated economies of Western Europe. And a succession of tax laws, monetary policies and other economic incentives programs lent encouragement to businesses seeking to invest money in nations overseas, setting up foreign subsidiaries, branches, factories and sales organizations.

The policy succeeded in an almost miraculous way. From 1945 to 1955 American firms invested $6.6 billion in overseas enterprises. From 1955 to 1965 the total was $20 billion. And from 1965 to 1974 the figure was $39 billion.

That investment built factories, introduced new technology and new marketing procedures, and created millions upon millions of jobs—mostly in Europe.

For a time, hardly anyone complained. Clearly the policy was morally correct (rebuilding the wreckage), politically advantageous (building up the economic strength of our allies) and economically sound (American unemployment remained low, few American factories were being closed, new markets were being developed).

But all that eventually changed. By the mid-1960s the European nations and Japan had made enormous economic gains. New factories and skilled energetic work forces could, and did, compete effectively with American workers. A dollar exchange rate fixed at an artificially high level made it even easier for Europeans and Japanese to underprice their American competitors. Scarcely hidden foreign government subsidies, export incentives and import restraints made the competitive situation worse for America. And Americans began grumbling about the "Uncle Sugar" approach to international economics.

The continuing investment by multinationals of tens of billions of dollars of American capital overseas, once seen as beneficial, seemed to be the crowning blow. Capital created by the productivity and innovativeness of Americans in America was being shipped overseas to build up-to-the-minute new factories in Stuttgart to compete with inefficient factories in Schenectady that were covered with the grime of thirty years' use.

Soon, machine tool plants in Schenectady were closed, shoe factories in Boston closed, and American workers were angry. The American labor movement began to have second thoughts about the blessings of "free trade." A trickle of worker complaints grew to tidal wave proportions. And the long-honored doctrine of "comparative advantage" was challenged. It made sense, union leaders said, in an open and fair world trading system, but not in a closed unfair trading system and certainly not in a one-way world investing system. The villain of the drama seemed apparent: the multinational corporation.

Of course, there were business counter-arguments, and we shall soon explore some of them. Capital invested overseas, businessmen noted, brought back to America a steady stream of profits, license fees and royalties—to a total of over $10 billion per year by 1976. Businessmen maintained that more Americans were employed, often newly employed, in export industries than were ever employed in those old shoe factories in Haverhill. They back up their claim with the latest data, showing clearly that America still exports more manufactured goods than it imports. Moreover, businessmen say, even outside the export field, the corporations that were creating the most jobs in the U.S. were actually American-based multinational corporations.

Still, the seed of discord and conflict had been planted. As a result of American capital investment, teen-aged girls in Taiwan were working at jobs once held by family men in Maine. All the statistics in the world cannot diminish the political implications of that fact, and the emotion-charged rhetoric and imagery flowing from it.

The Rise of OPEC

In October 1973, major Arab oil producers embargoed their product from the U.S. At the same time, the Organization of Petroleum Exporting Countries (OPEC) boosted oil prices, from $3.95 per barrel in January 1973 to $9.95 per barrel in January 1974, on the way to an official $23.50 per barrel in late-1979—and only the Lord knows how high in the post-Iranian revolution situation. In America, automobile owners waited on lines for hours to get five or ten gallons of gas—if they had odd-numbered license plates on odd-numbered days.

In the United States one oil company went out into the field with a camera crew to film reactions of customers as they inched their way to the fuel pumps. As the camera whirred, an interviewer asked, "Whose fault was the oil crisis?"

Was it the fault of the Congress? No, the customers replied. Was it the fault of the Israelis? No. The Arabs? No. America's wasteful consumption habits? No. Was it perhaps the fault of the oil companies? Damn right!

Of the ten largest industrial companies in the world, seven are oil companies. The second largest company (by sales volume) in the world, ranking behind General Motors, is Exxon, which in 1978 sold $60.3 billion worth of its products!

Oil companies are big companies. They are multinational companies. And despite at least some persuasive evidence to the contrary, American motorists perceived these big multinationals to be at fault for high gasoline prices and the long lines. If there was any doubt about it, the doubt was dispelled when oil companies' profits skyrocketed after the embargo. The fact that the companies claimed that the 400 percent rise in profits was essentially a one-time, technical occurrence—"inventory profits" is the accounting term for it—was almost irrelevant.

The villains seemed clear: the big multinational oil companies.

Third World Ploys

Third Worlders whooped with glee at the idea of underdeveloped nations causing discomfort to the capitalists of the West, even though the oil price increase may also have meant worse poverty and discomfort to their own people. The reaction was partly, but not wholly, emotional and symbolic. The imperialists were finally getting their comeuppance.

Behind the glee, however, was the seed of economic theory. If some underdeveloped nations could form a cartel dealing with oil and get away with quadrupling prices, why couldn't other underdeveloped nations form cartels dealing with copper, bauxite, tin, coffee, cocoa—almost any export commodity? And if they could do this, couldn't they reverse what they saw to be the cruel historical tide of Western economic imperialism, of Western economic exploitation, of Western economic rape?

Perhaps they could set up a New International Economic Order, an order that would, among other things, deal a mortal blow to that hateful instrument of economic imperialism—you guessed it— the multinational corporation. After all, Third Worlders asserted it was the MNCs that:

• exported excessive profits from the Third World nations,
• charged exorbitant license and royalty fees for already-developed technology,
• evaded tax liabilities,
• corruptly influenced governments and
• depleted the natural resources of the developing world.

The post-World War II revolution in communications technology in the poorer countries, beginning with radio and movies and continuing to the "magic lantern" of television, had spread awareness of widely different living standards throughout the electronic global village. This created a major political fact: the leaders who were demanding a New Order from the West were under pressure to deliver one, and quickly, at home. One target was obvious and easy, rich and fat: the multinational corporation.

The Corruption Issue

Stemming from investigation by the U.S. Senate Subcommittee on Multinational Corporations a series of business scandals were revealed:

- A giant multinational corporation, International Telephone and Telegraph, had apparently schemed with the Central Intelligence Agency to do political harm to Salvatore y Gossens Allende. (As it turned out, the ITT connection apparently had nothing to do with Allende's fall.)
- The Gulf Oil Corporation was buying political clout in Italy.
- The Lockheed Corporation was buying politicians in Japan, Holland, Iran and other nations around the world.
- Gulf, Ashland Oil, Hughes Tool, and Minnesota Mining and Manufacturing were also active closer to home, laying out massive sums of illegal campaign contributions, most of which went to Richard M. Nixon.
- Hundreds of U.S. companies ultimately informed the Securities and Exchange Commission that they had made "sensitive" or illegal payments overseas.

Businessmen responded in three basic ways. Some said it was a case of overpublicizing a few rotten apples in the barrel. Others said that, well, "everyone did it" in those strange foreign countries, and that when in Rome, or Teheran, or Amsterdam, one did as the native did or lose the business. A third group of businessmen said, simply, that it was terrible.

Western Reversals Around the World, Détente

Those same years that saw the rise of OPEC, the call for a New Economic Order, the perception of job export and the corruption scandals also saw another disturbing sequence of events, primarily political and military rather than economic.

In the decade and a half from 1965 to 1980, the Soviet Union gained military parity with the United States and began to strive for clearcut superiority. As the American influence receded, or seemed to recede, Soviet influence advanced, or seemed to advance, from Southeast Asia to Africa, and for a while to the Middle East.

In the aftermath of the Vietnam experience, many pundits noted that the United States had become militarily and politically over-extended. It was against this solemn backdrop that the global gamesmen Richard Nixon and Henry Kissinger announced "a new structure for peace." It was called "détente."

In its name, the Nixon administration decided that the Communists should be offered an increase in the amount of trade between the United States and the totalitarian Eastern bloc of nations. Not only was this a "carrot" for past (unmentioned) favors, it was also reasoned that further trade would encourage new Soviet steps toward better relations.

And so, trade restrictions with the Iron Curtain countries were relaxed. Items that were once considered of "strategic" value were declared not to be of strategic value. Accordingly, using Western technology, including American technology, the world's largest truck plant arose in the Soviet Union on the banks of the Kama River. Because of the generally poor condition of Russian roads, these will be extra-heavy-duty trucks. Of course, they will not be military trucks. The nations of the West aren't silly enough to provide the Soviet Union with the know-how to build a better military truck that can be sold and given away all over the world. These are civilian trucks. In order for them to be used for military purposes, why, they would have to be painted brown.

Seriously, a brave senior Commerce Department official has risked his career, and says he has suffered "bureaucratic reprisals," in order to warn Congress that the Soviet Union is diverting U.S. technology purchases from civilian to military purposes—and he specifically cites the $500 million worth of American technology, including IBM computers, installed in the Kama River truck plant. Laurence J. Brady, deputy director of the Commerce Department's Office of Export Administration, says that despite signed assurances from then-Secretary of State Kissinger and his Commerce superiors, as well as from the Soviets themselves, the Kama River plant's truck production is being diverted to military use. Brady accuses his bosses of deliberately misleading Congress by pretending they have upheld U.S. export control laws when they have actually gutted them.

Another official, Dr. Jack Vorona, assistant vice director for scientific and technical intelligence of the Defense Intelligence Agency, gave support to Brady's charges in congressional testimony. He said that some of the Kama River trucks are being used by the Soviet military, that some of the engines produced there may be winding up in other military vehicles, and that IBM 360 and 370 computers, instead of running the truck plant foundry as the Soviets promised, may have been secretly and illegally diverted to run the Warsaw Pact's air defenses.

So, as this sad tale illustrates, détente indeed turns out to be a one-way street, and the only result of incredibly shortsighted U.S. deals is a stronger, more dangerous U.S.S.R.

Other deals, or proposed deals, suggested the full ripeness of the Nixon-Kissinger policy. At a time when Arabs held a knife over the jugular of the Western world's supply of hydrocarbons, at a time when American industry was publicly worrying about capital shortages, at a time when interest rates were historically high, what did Nixon and Kissinger recommend? A $7 billion American investment, at government-subsidized low interest rates, to build a natural gas pipeline in Siberia, which eventually would supply Japan and the West Coast of the United States. The idea was to replace Western dependence on the Arabs, with Western dependence on the Soviet Union.

Of course, some good did come from the all-carrot, no-stick approach. President Nixon's crony Donald Kendall, president of Pepsico, set up a deal to sell Pepsi Cola to the Russians in return for the American distribution rights to Russian vodka. Peace, it's wonderful!

Consider then, two thoughts: Lenin's notion that the rope to hang the bourgeoisie would gladly be sold to the Soviet Union by the bourgeoisie, and Solzhenitsyn's thought that the West today would gladly sell earth-moving equipment to the Soviet Union to help in digging graves for the dissidents.

The Russians have always had a pungent sense of imagery, and when the same image recurs, first from a Communist, then half a century later from an anti-Communist, maybe there's a message there.

Well then: if the United States, and the West generally, are suffering hard times, and détente is one of the culprits, which are the instrumentalities that are accountable?

Well, who provided, or would provide, the technology for the truck plants, the computers for the KGB, the pipeline for Siberia, and the soft drinks so that the Russians can be debonair members of the Pepsi generation? Who provided all that nonmilitary technology that would allow the Soviets to divert their own capital and technology to embark on the most expensive peacetime military build-up in history? You guessed it: the multinationals. Guilty again!

Recession: The Decline of the Dollar

Even optimists, like at least one half of the present team of authors, concede ruefully that the 1970s have been somewhat less than boom-times. Two recessions (one a whopper), ongoing double-digit inflation, and a massive sinking spell in the value of the dollar combined to put the squeeze on the American standard of living. Real personal income had soared in the succulent sixties; real personal income did not soar in the sour seventies. Government data show that while real income did actually go up during the seventies, it went up at a much slower rate than in the sixties. Furthermore, the distortions of inflation allowed real incomes to drift upward for many but to plummet for others, particularly those most in need, most dramatically elderly Americans locked into fixed incomes. Finally, in a psychological sense, inflation robs us all. Even if our incomes are rising, we are bitterly convinced we would have more if inflation didn't pick our pockets, seldom realizing that one cause of our rising income is the inflationary spiral itself.

Economic hard times. Whose fault? The political dialogue is not noted for subtle and sophisticated distinctions. At a time of economic hardship, we look for, and find, villains closest to the economic action—big government, big labor, and big business. In the instance of big business, with a recent well-publicized history of corruption, of job export, of oil price spirals, the scrutiny was thorough and blame was indeed laid.

When the dollar did its nose dive in 1977 and 1978 whose fault was it? Well, there are many reasons of course, but there were all the American MNCs and banks dumping dollars all over the world, buying yen, francs and D-marks. Imagine: Americans making hay by selling America short! That there were some sound reasons for this activity not triggered by business, as we shall see, seemed almost irrelevant. Once again the MNCs were the bad guys.

The many strands come together: job export, OPEC, corruption, the New Economic Order, the flowering détente and Western economic reverses. As the strands come together, the result is a new defendant in the dock of the court of public opinion: the multinational corporation. The indictment is far-reaching and much publicized. Multinationals, we have heard, are really supranationals—so large, so powerful, so amoral, as to constitute a genuine threat to the nation state. Elected by no one, responsible to no one, caring only about fat black figures beneath the bottom line, we are told

that the new breed of messianic corporate conquerors regard themselves as the true heirs of Alexander and Napoleon, able to stitch
together a world fashioned to their own specifications.

Beyond that, we hear, the multinationals cheat on taxes; divulge
only misleading accounting statements; ravage the local resources
and environment; impose plastic Western values on traditional cultures; export too much capital from the home country, but also
pull too many profits away from the host country; actively engage
in corrupting governments; encourage war, imperialism and the
brain drain; steal technology from the rich countries, but charge
too much for it in the poor countries; and use child labor wherever
they can. The MNCs are said to be generally responsible for the
fact that some nations are well-to-do and some nations are poor,
that some people are well fed and others go hungry.

If Iran is in trouble, blame the multinationals. If Chilean Fascists
torture Chilean Communists, blame the MNCs. Some charges are
trivial, some plain wrong, some misstated and most exaggerated.
But some charges are serious and, indeed, profound, going to the
heart of the nature of our civilization.

It is our intent here to lay out several different, sincerely held
views on these issues. These views, as shall now be demonstrated,
are presented as though the parties in the debate were speaking for
themselves and for their interests.

As we go through this exercise our characters seek an answer to
a haunting question: "What kind of world do we want?" That, of
course, is the ultimate question for policy planners. As the reader
will note, it is a question that leads us to some remote and unex-
pected byways.

3.

A Businessman

I want to begin with a complaint. I want to say out loud what many of my fellow businessmen are thinking these days: We believe that we are the victims of a monstrous insult.

On balance, we businessmen believe multinational corporations have been uniquely effective instruments for transmitting well-being to every corner of the world. Indeed, we think we have created the most humanly beneficial system for producing and distributing goods and services ever known to man. Nothing more, nothing less. Accordingly, in this era when everything apparently must be seen as a contest between heroes and villains, we see ourselves in white hats.

Of course, the multinational issue is very complicated. But the results of our activity are obvious: our businesses have clearly led to a better life for countless billions of people around the world who live longer, live better, know more, are better housed and better clothed—all because of the existence and the expansion of the twentieth century American-style corporation.

Yet, strangely, we international businessmen are slandered around the world. We are accused of economic exploitation and political corruption; we are condemned for cultural imperialism and rape of resources, for the failure or the success of détente, for high oil prices, and for the dollar's erosion—you have just read the litany in the previous chapter.

Basically, we plead "not guilty." We so plead not because MNCs are perfect. They are not, nor are any other human institutions perfect. But if we are forced to reduce the case for MNCs to the simplest formulation we would say this:

> The multinational corporation symbolizes a system of international commerce that is better by far than what it replaced, which was nationalist, mercantilist and protectionist, a system that, in the 1930s, set nation against nation and ultimately played a role in the rending of the fabric of Western civilization.

> And this system of international commerce is better by far than what might replace it, which would be socialist, bureaucratic, overly regulated, nonentrepreneurial and less productive, a system that could easily make the 1980s a decade when the lights of economic creativity and human freedom dimmed—to all of our detriment.

There is nothing new about international commerce. We multinational businessmen may be the second oldest profession; in fact, some of our critics might maintain that we are really only the somewhat respectable branch of the oldest profession. Remember that, as early as 1200 B.C., the Phoenicians were busy traders known to their Mediterranean neighbors as the "merchants of the sea." Forerunners of the modern multinational corporation arose several centuries ago in the city-states of Italy and in the Low Countries. Such profit-seeking companies expanded the maritime empires of Spain, England and the Netherlands, and helped settle the New World. Some entrepreneurs were traders who hoped to make fortunes on a few voyages. But others were "direct investors," with a longer perspective, and they helped build settlements like Jamestown and New Amsterdam. These transnational enterprises did not prevent national rivalries and wars, but they did advance civilization around the world, as they still do.

You ask: "What kind of world do we want?" Businessmen want a world where increased prosperity leads to increased stability and greater world harmony. Businessmen aren't supposed to be great visionary idealists, but remember, it was a businessman, legendary by now, who said it best. "One World" is what Wendell Willkie pleaded for.

Do multinationals lead to the goal? They do indeed. It's happening. An economic "One World" now exists. The world is becoming a single information and technological system and a single economic trading unit. The politicians have surely failed to organize a Parliament of Man at the United Nations—as demonstrated by the craven bickering that passes for debate at Turtle Bay. But we businessmen have succeeded far better than we realize in creating a single world marketplace. Travel, communications, technical and cultural exchange, all arising from multinational business, are knitting the earth together in a new way. From their common commercial activity comes a shared perspective that makes the businessmen of different nations more like each other than their countrymen. Throughout the world, consumers, too, are drawn together by shared tastes and the common benefits of higher productivity and lower real costs for goods and services.

Historian Arnold Toynbee, in a 1974 interview, offered a typically cosmic conception of what is happening: "Sovereignty on a local scale is an illusion because you can't be economically independent locally. . . . Actually there are already world citizens running the world's economy because there isn't a world state to run it. I think this is the way a world political organization is going to come into existence. It is going to be anticipated by a world economic organization."

There is a great irony afoot in the world. There has been so much talk about radicalism and idealism in the world during this last decade. But the real radicals and idealists, the people leading us to the sunlit uplands, are businessmen!

One of my business colleagues, Irving S. Shapiro, chairman of the board of E.I. DuPont de Nemours and Company, described his view of the world a few years ago in this striking way:

> Politically, the world is fragmented; it always has been and, short of a miracle, it always will be. I accept that as a fact of life, but I am a devoted and optimistic advocate of what I call one-world economics. There are no geographical boundaries to the needs of people and no justification in morals or ethics for some nations to be haves and others to be have-nots.

Mr. Shapiro's advocacy does not take place in a vacuum. He has a goal in mind:

> One-world economics envisions worldwide needs as a worldwide market and the worldwide business structure as a resource for meet-

ing its needs. It is an escalation of national economic systems and attitudes to a global scale. . . . Unlike one-world politics, one-world economics is within reach. The productive system is proven out, and much of it is in place. What remains is to harness it effectively to the worldwide task.

What remains, in other words, is the same task of global unification that politics and politicians have been shirking and failing to accomplish for centuries. As the momentum of events sweeps us along, many of my thoughtful business colleagues believe we may slip back toward the kind of world that two generations ago deepened depression by building economic walls, and then drifted into war. The politicians are failing, not the businessmen; the world is backsliding because the idea of political integration has proved impossible and politicians have no other vision with which to replace it.

There is another irony evident in the world today. At just the time when it can be demonstrated that politics is failing to give us the kind of world we want, and at just the time when it can be demonstrated that business is helping to give us the kind of world we want, we are faced with an incredible assault by politicians upon businessmen! No wonder we feel insulted!

A half dozen years ago, N.R. Danielian, then president of the International Economic Policy Association, eloquently described the plight of the multinational corporations to a Congressional committee:

> There is no other instrumentality with the same flexibility, inventiveness, initiative and effectiveness as the multinational corporation in undertaking the extraction, refinement, fabrication, transportation and marketing (of the world's) resources. No armies, no government, no foreign aid, no international institutions can match this achievement. . . . (Yet) they (multinational companies) are confronted with a diversity of political motivation—some of emotional origin, such as nationalism; others ideological, such as consumerism; and some even humanitarian, as in the case of welfarism. . . . Multinational corporations, the most important instrument of economic development, are . . . buffeted by the violent currents of world politics, with no support in public opinion, no court of appeal, and often abandoned by their own governments.

He said, "abandoned"—and that's the correct word.
Now we must ask ourselves other questions: How and why does

the MNC help bring about a better world? We businessmen ought to be asking and answering that question regularly. For if we can explain some basic principles, and some roots of basic antagonisms, it will be apparent that so many of the criticisms of MNCs are misguided.

Let me begin by noting that no tears need be shed for the "abandoned" MNCs that Mr. Danielian refers to. They are much too powerful to be pitied; in that sense our critics are correct.

It is, however, important to understand just why the multinational corporations are so powerful (and so controversial). Several reasons come to mind:

- They are both large and rationally organized in a world full of large, inefficient and more or less totally disorganized entities, many of them governmental.
- They are typically successful in carrying out their ambitions, plans and projects, in contrast to the dismal record of the government-planned economies.
- They pay their workers more, and the managers considerably more, than their counterparts in the local economies of the countries in which they operate (often triggering the emotion of envy).
- They are far more credit-worthy, in the eyes of both national and international lenders, than typically hard-pressed governments (often intensifying the envy reaction).
- They are sources of innovation and change, often of a radical kind, and thus they upset cozy, settled power structures and establishments.
- They are ingenious enough to legally keep at least one jump ahead of slow moving but resentful government tax collectors and regulators.

In short, they work. Their power, their ubiquity and the controversy they engender can perhaps be best gauged by one statistic. According to an estimate made in 1970 and now doubtless too low, U.S.-based multinationals have created 8,000 subsidiaries throughout the world! These subsidiaries have a combined output greater than that of any nation except the U.S., the U.S.S.R. or Japan.

I say that MNCs work well. Most of my business associates agree with me. They produce and distribute goods and services better than any other instrumentality known to man. Their activity directly helps hungry rural peasants, favela-dwelling migrants in shanties, sick people all over the developing world, as well as hundreds of millions of middle-class people in the industrial world.

What is their ultimate secret? How do they achieve their wondrous results? It is both elementary and crass: the pursuit of profits.

The pursuit of profit is the universal motivation of private business enterprise. It is the mainspring of economic progress. This is true whether the enterprise is a tiny corner grocery store or a giant corporation operating on a global scale. Because "profit" is a fighting word in contemporary discussion of business and politics, a brief digression is in order to define the role that profits play.

Economist Paul Samuelson provides an entertaining definition that shows how profits work:

> Profits . . . are the carrots dangled before us enterprising donkeys. Losses are our penalty kicks. Profits go to those who (are) efficient in making things, in selling things, in foreseeing things. Through profits, society is giving command over new ventures to those who have piled up a record of success.

It is important to understand that the people reward efficient producers for their skills at supplying what the people want. The reward is profit. The system is efficient. And the party left out of the process is the government. Therein lies the root of the unending argument between the businessman/capitalist and the politician/bureaucrat: Who shall have the last word? In most countries, other than the U.S., the government has long since had the final word. Businessmen may do well for themselves, and perhaps incidentally do well for their customers, only so long as they do what they are told by government.

Much of the fierce opposition to the MNCs from foreign politicians and intellectuals is the same old domestic anti-business argument cast anew in global terms. Whether in Washington, Mexico City or Tokyo, the ambitious politician, the leftist intellectual and the senior government bureaucrat are convinced that they should regulate the marketplace and make the choices to "protect" unenlightened consumers. They believe that they and not selfish businessmen should be in charge of defining and providing for "the public good." Papa knows best. Once governments believe that, they will entertain and encourage and stimulate a hundred different arguments against MNCs, all with the ultimate aim of harnessing, muzzling, restricting and ultimately directing operations. That is not abstract theory. It has happened. It continues to happen. I know it happens; my colleagues in the corporate world know it happens. We have felt the sting of the lash; we have been harnessed, muzzled, restricted and directed.

But as we know, and as most economists know, private, profit-seeking enterprise on the American model is most productive and socially rewarding in a setting of fairly wide-ranging individual freedoms, especially the consumer's freedom to choose in the economic marketplace. When governments step in to dominate the marketplace and to "protect" consumers from profit-motivated businessmen, they actually rob consumers of their free choice. Governments want steel mills; consumers want cars. When governments take over you get unneeded inefficient steel mills and few cars. The dead hand of government regulation and superplanning slows down the creative juices that are stimulated by Samuelson's "dangling carrots" of profits. And everyone suffers, as we've seen in the sorry performances of heavily regulated economies all over the world.

There is another factor that sets up an anti-MNC bias among so many governments. The freewheeling marketplace economies of MNCs, from America and other nations, lead almost inevitably toward a more open society, the freeing up of social arrangements, and ultimately a diffusion of power. A free marketplace can yield freer politics. Papa-knows-best governments don't like that.

So much for theory. But we businessmen are practical people. Let's now take a look at how the MNCs, those profit-making, people-helping, world-shaping beasts, function in actual practice. For some grave misconceptions have come into the public dialogue, and if we are to deal intelligently with the phenomenon we should understand what is myth and what is fact.

Let us consider, briefly, five broad categories of multinational enterprises. Divided by function, they are:

1. Labor-intensive (e.g., shoes, textiles)
2. Low-technology (autos, consumer electronics)
3. High-technology (jet aircraft, computers)
4. Extractive (oil, mining)
5. Services, especially in banking and finance

Manufacturing Multinationals

The first three categories represent manufacturing companies.

Contrary to popular mythology as conveyed by the book *Global Reach* and other myth-mongering works, the prototypical manufacturing MNC is not engaged in trying to make a quick buck by exploiting sweatshop labor in, say, ladies shoes or men's clothing for export back to the U.S. Whatever the case may have been a generation or even a decade ago, the quick-buck game no longer pays off very often.

Why not? For one thing, wage differentials between the U.S. and other countries continue to narrow. For another, "floating" exchange rates can create major uncertainties for quick-buck operators counting pennies.

Although the "runaway" shoe or textile plant has often become a dubious economic venture, it still exists. Its impact is small, however. This will be recognized if we keep in mind a single statistic: more than eighty-two percent of American multinational investment goes to developed nations where wage rates are now roughly equal to wage rates in America. You can't buy sweatshop labor in West Germany or Canada any more than you can buy it in America. Unions are strong in both places and a vast infrastructure of social welfare legislation exists in both places. If there is evidence that we businessmen are succeeding in curtailing union power around the world, I'd sure like to see it. It might help my digestion.

What about the other eighteen percent? That is invested in nations where wage rates are relatively low. Most of this investment (better than eighty cents of every dollar) is invested in Latin America, the most developed of the less-developed nations, and where the U.S. has long-standing economic ties. But, in any event, a great deal of U.S. investment in developing countries is in the extractive industries—oil, copper, tin, bauxite and so on. And those industries are located overseas not because of cheap labor but because it has been discovered that to mine tin it is useful to go where tin is. In all, probably no more than eight percent of America's overseas direct investment is placed in low-wage nations for the purpose of manufacturing goods. Insofar as it's a problem, it's a small problem.

Moreover, many foreign-based MNCs, whose home countries once were considered sources of "sweatshop" labor threatening American jobs and living standards, now come to the U.S. to build with American labor the products they sell to Americans. For example, Sony, a truly pioneering MNC, has established two television set plants in the U.S., and it is building another plant to manufacture video tape recorders. Rather than continue exports from Japan, Sanyo, which bought Whirlpool's TV set subsidiary in Chicago, will build its color television receivers there—a move other Japanese manufacturers are expected to follow.

There is a general principle at work here: manufacturing facilities, representing substantial fixed investments, inevitably follow expanding markets. It is not generally the relatively low-paid worker who attracts the direct investor; it is the increasingly better-paid consumer. And intense competition for the consumer's favor often will force a foreign investor to enter into manufacturing to protect a threatened share of the market. A prime example: Volkswagen's long-delayed, soul-wrenching but unavoidable decision to invest in a large U.S. assembly plant, which will eventually employ 2,500 American workers. This decision was made unavoidable because of Volkswagen's shrinking share of the American auto market, which in turn was related to the fact that by 1975 unit labor costs in West Germany were greater than in the U.S. With the subsequent dive of the dollar, the situation worsened from the point of view of a German manufacturer trying to sell a Beetle at a reasonable cost.

What is mostly true for many labor-intensive and low-technology industries is almost entirely true for high-technology (capital intensive) industries.

The computer company does not go overseas to find cheap labor to build computers. Not that much labor is required. Even electric typewriters made by IBM can be efficiently produced by highly automated plants in the United States and then sold competitively overseas.

In fact, IBM builds plants overseas for an entirely different reason: that's the only way they can capture a share of the foreign market. For notwithstanding all the incessant talk about free market and the lowering of tariff walls, the Japanese and most European governments make it very difficult for a large foreign company to do business on their soil unless they also do some manufacturing there.

Is all this foreign manufacturing, of both labor-intensive and capital-intensive modes, good for the kind of world we Americans want? Is it good for the kind of America we want? We businessmen believe it is.

Even in those remaining instances where "cheap labor" is still the lure, the products that come back to the U.S. are sold to American consumers at lower prices, reducing inflationary pressures. That was the original classical argument for Smith-ian "comparative advantage": cheaper prices for all. Every time an American workingman buys a foreign-made bicycle or a baseball glove or a radio or a television set, he proves one thing: *Smith lives.* Because his theories live, we all live better lives, able to buy more goods with a dollar.

Of course, multinational enterprise does more than that. In essence, it enables ever greater numbers of people to share in the creativity of the most innovative forces of civilization. That surely is one of the central benefits of international commerce: to avoid massive and wasteful duplication of effort. If IBM spends twenty years developing a computer, does it follow that every nation wanting or needing a computer must spend twenty years developing one? No sir, nor will they. If we don't license our subsidiaries to produce those goods overseas on reasonable terms, technology transfer, if you will, that technology will be pilfered and the international agreements concerning patents and copyright wouldn't be worth the paper they're printed upon. And that is *not* the kind of world we want to live in! That is anarchy.

Extractive Multinationals

If we multinational businessmen are generally not guilty of seeking "cheap" labor overseas, we are still commonly accused of "exploiting" the natural resources of the developing countries. That, too, is bunk. Such criticisms of MNCs in the extractive industries reflect ignorance of the actual flow of U.S. overseas investment and the realities of large-scale international resource development. Moreover, contrary to the widely accepted myth, most of the world's raw materials are extracted from the economically advanced countries rather than the less-developed countries (LDCs). If resource-rape is going on, it is at least legitimized by being a backyard as well as a far away activity.

The facts of resource investment reveal an interesting pattern. Far from being forced to repel avaricious foreigners lusting after their natural riches, developing nations are often competing vigorously for investment funds that might otherwise be destined for consumer markets of Western Europe, Japan and other advanced countries.

For the truth is that big profits with smaller risks come from investing in stable nations with large and expanding consumer markets. Raw material development is quite a different matter. The chances of failure on a grand scale in bringing in a new oil field or opening a new copper mine are quite large, especially in unstable developing countries. Anticapitalist and antiforeigner politics in many of the LDCs usually make them unattractive places to risk large amounts of capital. Such countries are often dangerous mine-fields, laying in wait to blow up promising managerial careers—one more reason that executives may just as soon invest in Europe or Canada.

And yet such high-risk gambles are made, and, with a bit of luck, pay off handsomely. For example, Papua, New Guinea, one of the world's newest (and most backward) nations, owes its very existence and tenuous economic viability to the huge, partly government-owned copper mine on Bougainville Island. The third largest open-pit mine in the world, it is a $450 million plus enterprise undertaken by British and Australian MNCs, financed by an American-led international banking consortium, and based on long-term supply contracts with Japanese and European copper users. True internationalism! To give some idea of that one mine's importance to the Papua, New Guinea economy, the annual sales of the mine's output, depending on the world price of copper, represent one-half to two-thirds of the country's total export earnings.

The success of Bougainville Copper Ltd. illustrates the observation of the Chase Bank's David Rockefeller: "The real contribution of a multinational company to a developing economy is its ability to mobilize local resources—capital, raw materials and human capabilities—in a way that will trigger more growth in the domestic economy." With the boost from Bougainville Copper, Papua, New Guinea has literally jumped from the Stone Age to the Jet Age. The mine's construction and continuing apprentice program are responsible for the training of most of the nation's carpenters, electricians, welders and heavy equipment operators. Other major development projects—hydropower, mining, industrialization, tourism—are being pursued by the government and private, multinational investors. If it remains attractive to private investment, Papua, New Guinea has the potential to become one of the economic development showcases of the Pacific Basin.

The Bougainville mine also illustrates the often neglected investor's side of risky multinational enterprise. I've been on that side and, believe me, the risks are enormous. For example, there is no way that the banks can repossess a half-billion dollar hole in the ground if the government demands a renegotiation of the original deal. That actually happened in Papua, New Guinea. Against the background of a plummeting copper price that threatened all of them, the company, the bankers and the government, with admirable realism, negotiated a new formula. As a result, the investment climate is now deemed attractive enough to encourage new large-scale mining investment.

A captive copper mine is an extreme example of contemporary investment reality: there are no longer any one-night stands, and every businessman knows it. Once an MNC, or a consortium of MNCs, commits itself to a developing country and assumes the political-economic risks of a multimillion-dollar direct investment, it is usually there for at least as long as the tenure of the key corporate decision-makers, whose judgment is thereafter bound up with the project. (Businessmen—surprise!—have big egos. And executive ego and pride are powerful, little recognized determinants of corporate behavior.)

Contrary to leftist mythology, the governments of the Third World usually succeed in imposing their will on captive MNCs and wind up exploiting them. It is not the other way around. The hole in the ground remains in the Third World no matter what. That's a pretty strong fact to open a negotiation with.

Where Third World governments do lose out is when they demand too much, too soon, thereby sacrificing expected benefits. For example, not long ago Kennecott Copper Corporation, after two years of research, identified a large government-controlled, low-grade copper deposit on Baja California in Mexico as worthy of serious study and negotiation. The project would be in the $300 million plus class if it materialized. The deposit posed special metallurgical difficulties and would require the use of Kennecott's proprietary technology to recover the ore. With Mexico's major government-controlled copper projects far behind schedule, this offered a badly needed way to expedite development and meet future supply targets. But before Kennecott could take the first step toward a proposal, the Mexican government announced ultra-nationalist and restrictive new laws affecting foreign investment and technology transfer. Kennecott decided to abandon the project and seek copper in a more hospitable political-economic climate. The big loser: Mexico, demanding too much, too soon.

The relationship between a multinational company and a host country government is never simple anywhere, but as we businessmen have learned, it is especially complex and sensitive in the developing world. As former Secretary of State Kissinger has declared: "Transnational enterprises have been powerful instruments of modernization in the developing nations where there is no substitute for their ability." It is precisely this fact, expertise and know-how, as much as their wealth and power, that makes the MNCs objects of a love-hate relationship on the part of proud Third Worlders. The less developed nations want to do it all their own way. Unfortunately, it doesn't work very well their way; that is one big reason less-developed nations are less-developed. Multinational business is not just a matter of profits and losses; national pride is deeply involved and skilled MNC managers try to take it into account.

In past generations weak and pliable governments in some backward countries allowed themselves to be bullied and even bought by large foreign companies, first European and later American. Such bribery, unfortunately, remains a way of life even though many governments in LDCs have grown stronger and therefore theoretically more capable of resisting temptation. That hasn't happened; now, in fact, they are frequently the active initiators of the bribery process, as recent investigations have shown.

We businessmen, in fact, face a new dilemma. As the dollar declined we have been pushed by the U.S. government to export more to help right America's negative balance of trade. Fine. Except we are also told that we cannot operate by the locally prevalent rules: a consultants fee here, a payoff there. But the German MNCs and the French MNCs have no such qualms. And they then get the orders. The jobs go to Germany and France. And America gets a bigger trade deficit. Wonderful!

In any event, we businessmen know that the image of an overbearing United Fruit Company dictating terms to the puppet leaders of a banana republic is exceptional and, in fact, anachronistic. Nowadays, the local government does the economic dictating, sometimes with the help of high-powered United Nations and World Bank consultants who know how to drive a hard bargain. Spurred on by the example of OPEC's humbling of the once mighty oil companies, developing countries are steadily negotiating a bigger share of MNCs' profits, jobs and markets, as well as more favorable access to managerial skills and technological know-how. For example, in the field of technology transfer, several Latin American countries have slashed the royalty fees paid for MNCs' technical design and trademark licenses, a move these countries justify by complaints against alleged past overchargings.

Developing countries are also imposing other economic goals on

MNCs. For example, the Andean Pact countries—Colombia, Venezuela, Chile, Peru, Bolivia and Ecuador—insist that foreign investors export eighty percent of their products outside the regional group or face the seizure of their property. Their thought was that these structures would guarantee the Andeans a big step toward a more favorable balance of trade.

Does this intimidation work? Only when exercised delicately and skillfully. By no coincidence, new foreign investment in the Andean Pact countries has lagged, and now some member nations are openly competing for capital on more flexible terms.

The once-mighty MNCs have only one countervailing power these days. It was expressed rather well in a November 1973 statement to the U.S.'s "Group of Eminent Persons" studying the impact of multinational corporations. Sir Val Duncan, chairman of the Rio Tinto-Zinc Corporation Ltd., declared: "The power of most multinational corporations in the world is much exaggerated. They do have one well-defined authority, however, and that is the power not to invest if they do not wish to do so."

Most of my colleagues in the business community have learned that lesson the hard way; we have been pushed, shoved, squeezed and harassed, and we cannot really do likewise in return. All we can do is nothing—we can withhold cooperation or investment. But sooner or later, the message actually gets through; the countries need us as much as we need them.

Banking Multinationals

A word is in order here about the key role that multinational banks play in the new international economy. They are responsible for the healthy circulation of the system's lifeblood—investment capital. They see to it, simply, that money does useful things. They operate in ways that shatter the old-fashioned stereotype of the stuffy ultraconservative banker who wouldn't lend you money unless you really didn't need it. In the international sphere where national regulatory restrictions touch them lightly if at all, the banking MNCs are sometimes radically innovative in their dealmaking because they have to be. Admittedly, this can be risky. Bankrolling oil drilling in the storm-tossed North Sea is not a job for a man with no nerve. But new forms of higher rolling have enabled banking to modernize itself and to keep pace with a fast-changing world. It has also been essential to the difficult task of "recycling" petro-dollars from OPEC to oil-consuming countries by means of bank lending on a massive scale.

According to the Federal Reserve Board, major foreign branches of U.S. commercial banks had more than $208 billion in outstanding loans at the end of 1978, compared to $686 billion in domestic loans. That's quite a hefty proportion. These figures include loans to government and corporations, as well as funds placed with other banks.

An air of mystery surrounds banking, and international bankers are seen as shadowy figures whose machinations seldom add up to good for ordinary people. A prime source of unwarranted mystery and suspicion is the so-called Eurodollar market. A "Eurodollar" is simply a dollar on deposit in a commercial bank outside the U.S., usually in a major money center such as London. Eurodollars exist in abundance—an estimated $500 billion are in circulation. The currency is in dollars because the bulk of the world's trade has been denominated in dollars since the early postwar period, and foreigners (at least until the past decade or so) have preferred to hold dollars rather than other currencies.

These Eurodollars are truly global money, a freemarket pool of capital to be lent and invested anywhere, by anyone who possesses them, with a minimum of government regulation and interference. Naturally, this infuriates the would-be regulators and their political sponsors. But the borrowers, among them the developing countries, are not heard complaining about the existence of the Eurodollar market. Without it, they would have to go begging from one nation to another for government-approved loans. More generally, without multinational banks the ongoing process of development around the world would come to a screeching halt. And those "ordinary people" who like to beat up on bankers as much as they like to pummel the rest of us businessmen would be the most grievously hurt.

What is the answer to the ongoing war of nerves between the MNCs and their critics? Pierre Drouin has written in *Le Monde:* "Economic, social, cultural and political ends are closely linked in the development process, and the multinational firms promote only the economic side. . . . The first rule should be to harmonize from the outset as closely as possible the multinational firm's 'private plans' with the national plan so that foreign investments can be managed in the closest possible conformity with national policies."

Easy to say. Harmony. But businessmen know that such harmony may in practice mean government direction and outright control. For Drouin assumes the existence of a government-planned economy and official resource allocation. This is the fate that those of us who operate multinational companies hope to avoid. In an April 1975 study prepared for the U.S. Department of State, the International Management and Development Institute reported: "In conducting our study of corporate opinion . . . no other priority emerged with such urgency as the need for corporations to remain independent of *all* political pressures and persuasions."

There is all the difference in the world between Ford Motor Company and its dealers embarking voluntarily on a program of grade-school building in low income rural areas of Mexico and Argentina—more than 100 schools have been built—and a company being ordered by a government to divert resources to social projects, as is the case in socialist Peru. Ford wants to be a good corporate citizen, but not an instrument of any government, including the government of the United States of America. The proper way to do these things, as businessmen see it, is to let business have freedom, let it make profits from that freedom, and *then* let the government tax away a share of profits for whatever purposes it deems valuable. Render unto Caesar.

Such freedom, history has shown, more than pays its way. In those developing countries that give MNCs considerable investment freedom and operating flexibility, progress is stunning—and not merely in economic terms. Consider the situation of the peasant who becomes a well-paid employee of an MNC. His whole world suddenly expands. His living standard soars. His health improves. His children are more likely to attend school and achieve literacy. All as a result of the job created by MNC risk-taking and initiative.

For example, in a depressed region of Brazil, Champion International planted 75 million trees in a dozen years, creating an entirely new pulp and paper industry. A decade ago, the first workers walked barefoot to the mill. Today, all but three of the 1,400 employees are Brazilians, and workers' cars fill the parking lot to overflowing. Such examples of dramatic progress through MNC investment can be found throughout the Third World, frequently in the extractive and natural resource sectors.

Of course, there are some comfortably situated critics of the MNCs, who wear imported shoes and drive imported cars, who would be sure to seize upon the crowded employee parking lot in the boondocks of Brazil as a despicable symbol of "Yankee cultural imperialism" and "gross, materialistic aggression" against the quaint natives. These abstract hate-words have nothing to do with the peasants of Brazil and everything to do with the guilt hangups of leftist intellectuals. To the Brazilian peasant, a job in the paper mill is not merely a pair of shoes or a car. It is literacy and longer life expectancy and better housing and enhanced human dignity—all without any necessary sacrifice of his cultural identity.

The multinational corporation may actually improve and enhance the traditional agricultural way of life in a developing country. Years ago, the Firestone Tire and Rubber Company invested in the development of rubber plantations in Liberia. As a sideline, the company started raising chickens. When the Liberians showed an interest, Firestone taught them how to run chicken-raising farms—the beginning of a thriving new poultry business for the country. Firestone eventually gave up chicken-raising, depending on the local suppliers they helped train. The company's researchers also set up Liberia's first cattle-breeding program and botanical experiments that led to the introduction of new tropical fruits and plants. By ranging afield, Firestone helped the Liberians and strengthened its position as a foreign investor.

You authors say that MNCs are in the dock of public opinion, and, of course, in that you are correct—whether we deserve to be there or not. Nowhere is this more evident than in regard to the so-called "corruption" issue.

Businessmen know that in a world in which politics increasingly dominates economics, the abuses of political power are inevitable. We have learned that government officials, armed with arbitrary and often plenary power, easily succumb to the temptation to turn their offices to advantage and extort bribes from favor-seeking businessmen.

Thus, disclosures of widespread U.S. corporate bribery overseas, highlighted by the Lockheed Aircraft Corporation's payoffs in Japan and Italy, are scarcely surprising. In many countries, including some considered "advanced," the practice is well established of paying "consulting" fees and commissions to government officials (or their nominees) in return for assistance of various kinds. This is certainly the case in Japan and Italy. To say that "everyone" engages in such bribery doubtless goes too far, but European and Japanese businessmen exposed to the same pressures as their American competitors have made the expected payments without being exposed to a moral inquisition at home.

The American public's reaction to the payoff scandals is one of sincere disapproval based on utter ignorance of the seamy underside of world trade. The reaction of the news media was predictable. Here is a follow-up story to Watergate—Businessgate!—and

full of all the predictable stereotypes. Unfortunately, sensation-
alized exposes of "business corruption" condemn all businessmen
for the questionable practices of a relative few.

But the reaction of morally posturing politicians, whose outrage
begins only at the water's edge, is especially interesting. John J.
McCloy, the lawyer-statesman who is the presumptive head of the
American Establishment, conducted a nine-month investigation
into Gulf Oil Corporation's illegal political activities that resulted
in the dismissal of the firm's chairman and two other top executives. McCloy is offended by the hypocritical double standard evident in Washington's reaction. He believes that it was "just as
improper" for American politicians to accept illegal corporate contributions as it was for businessmen to give them.

Some leading international businessmen cannot contain their
moral contempt for the politicians who are using phony antibusi-
ness arguments to attract media attention and votes. David Rockefeller, for one, demands to know: "Why doesn't the government
support the multinational corporations rather than trying to destroy them? It would be better if the government simply left them
alone instead of berating them at every opportunity."

Walter Wriston, chairman of Citicorp, echoes Rockefeller's complaint and declares, in so many words, that "Washington poses a
greater threat to free enterprise than Moscow does."

Some executives of highly exposed MNCs feel betrayed and
abandoned by their own government. This is especially true of executives of Gulf who thought their secret cash contributions to the
South Korean government were "in conformity with" U.S. government policy, or the ITT executives who thought the government
would welcome their help in undercutting the extreme leftist Allende regime in Chile.

In general, American MNCs, while they resist being used as de-
liberate instruments of U.S. foreign policy, wonder why they cannot have the same kind of official support that their European and
Japanese counterparts (and competitors) enjoy while operating in
foreign markets and reducing the risks of investment in developing
countries. They are not asking for special treatment, but merely
diligent protection of their rights under international law. "If the
U.S. properly protected these rights," says a former high (Republican) government economic policymaker, "it would do a great deal
for our foreign policy."

There is a great deal of talk, and some long-awaited action about
"codes of conduct" for multinational enterprises. The Organization

for Economic Cooperation and Development is negotiating such a code. Respected private organizations such as the Conference Board are drawing up codes that may prove realistic and workable because they are based on real-life business situations and experiences. Such studies are long overdue, and may help clear the air. Even more useful would be a situation where politicians and media stopped sensationalizing and started examining the complex realities of international business.

It is not only politicians who anger us these days. We are equally incensed at the phony arguments made by U.S. labor unions. They are as responsible as anyone for bringing multinational business into the dock of public opinion—and they should know better.

Consider, for example, the claim that American multinational corporations are engaged in "exporting" jobs. Untrue. Actually, far from "exporting" jobs, U.S.-based multinational corporations create hundreds of thousands of additional jobs at home. They do so by stimulating and expanding the exports of American goods to other countries. Remember that each additional billion dollars of exports creates about 60,000 additional jobs. Rarely considered in the ongoing argument is that a considerable part of U.S. trade each year is between domestic and foreign branches of the same multinational corporation. A manufacturer may typically produce component parts in the U.S., export them to its own foreign subsidiary, where they will be assembled, along with local components, into final products.

World trade looms ever larger in the U.S. economy. In 1978, exports accounted for 9.7 percent of the GNP and about 5 percent of employment—some 4 million jobs. Moreover, as we will see, in recent years the trade-related portion of the U.S.'s GNP has been the most dynamic and rewarding sector of the economy in terms of jobs and wages.

Of course, imports do affect U.S. companies and workers. In recent years, the U.S. has lost substantial parts of entire industries—apparel, shoes, bicycles, radios—to foreign competitors. The unions demand that tariff and quota walls be built to "protect" these jobs. But this only invites retaliation. When we attempt to close our markets to consumer imports, foreign nations affected by our moves respond in kind, or they discriminate against our industrial exports. Protectionism is self-defeating. To get back to our original proposition: that is not the kind of world we want to live in, nation fighting nation, all deeply embroiled in politicizing decisions about whether or not bicycles can be imported. The healthiest economy for all is one that is left to seek its own best efficiencies.

Only such a flexible system can respond to the fast-changing world economy marked by the free movement of people, ideas, money and goods. In such an economy we find that political and economic problems are subject to rapid redefinition. A self-correcting system exists, and it is essentially healthy. For example, a half dozen years ago, American textile manufacturers were complaining to Washington that they would be ruined by "cheap" Japanese imports. "Voluntary" quotas were imposed on Japanese textiles. Currency exchange rates between the dollar and the yen were then adjusted, which helped shift the balance. But the real breakthrough came from another source: Japanese young people demanded the same trendy clothes, especially blue jeans, as their American counterparts. Soon, the exports and fortunes of San Francisco-based Levi Strauss and Co. soared, prompting Japanese textile manufacturers to complain to Tokyo against the "flood" of American imports invading their market.

And, surprise, it is the Japanese textile industry that is now permanently depressed by "cheap" imports from low-wage developing countries—like Taiwan, the Philippines and Thailand. But the Japanese government does not intend to protect this "sunset" industry which has become uncompetitive. Instead, government energy is being directed at systematically shifting human and capital resources to more efficient and competitive "sunrise" industries. That's one form of government economic activity that makes sense!

Contrary to protectionist propaganda, the U.S. is holding its own, thank you, in export competition. In 1976, the U.S. accounted for 18.1 percent of total world exports of manufactured goods, compared with 19.1 percent for West Germany, 14.8 percent for Japan and 8.5 percent for Great Britain. After a prolonged decline, caused in large measure by an overvalued dollar that made U.S. exports less competitive, the trend has reversed and the U.S. share of world exports of manufactured goods is at least stable and probably increasing. We still export far more manufactured goods than we import. That fact stems essentially from the creative and innovative activity of those terrible boogeymen—multinationals.

During the decade from the mid-1960s to the mid-1970s, trade-related employment in the U.S. increased at an annual rate of 8.7 percent, compared to an annual increase of only one percent in the domestic economy as a whole. These are better paying jobs, too.

Workers employed in export-related industries are estimated to receive average wages about twenty-five percent higher than those whose activities are purely domestic. Wages have risen because these are high growth industries. Indeed, it is a little known but highly significant fact that exports are growing more rapidly than U.S. production of goods for U.S. consumption. And multinational corporations account for roughly half of total U.S. exports. Obviously, instead of penalizing them, U.S. government policy should encourage the companies that serve growing export markets and create high quality jobs.

The unions and their political allies accept the "exports-equal-jobs" equation without difficulty. They know that exports keep our factories humming. But they blindly—and, too often, irrationally—oppose U.S. captial investment and production in foreign countries. They claim that the outflow of capital and technology drains away the vitality of the American economy, stunting its future growth potential. Some union-oriented economists and academics go so far as to draw dubious parallels between the U.S. and England, attributing the latter's decline in large part to excessive foreign investment. (In my judgment, when you consider the record of British unions in crippling that nation's economy, the "flight" of British capital, if such it was, can be more properly credited to a survival instinct.)

But foreign trade and foreign investment are complementary activities in the global marketplace. They are inextricably bound together. Most of the U.S. private investment abroad is made by large international companies which are also active in trade. For a variety of reasons, they often have not had and do not have a real choice between exporting goods from the U.S. and producing them abroad. And businessmen understand, even if no one else seems to, that the bottom line judgment on the net benefits of such foreign investment is nowhere near as obvious as the protectionist unions would have us believe.

Unquestionably, U.S. foreign investment has grown rapidly. Between 1960 and 1975, the value of the U.S. investments abroad quadrupled to $120 billion. Such investment continues apace today—notwithstanding all the talk (and some reality) about foreigners "buying up America."

Why did overseas investment boom? One big reason, no longer operative, is that U.S. government policy had the effect of encouraging foreign investment during the 1960s and early 1970s by keeping the dollar overvalued. Under those circumstances, a dollar invested overseas bought much more plant and equipment there than it did at home.

Those U.S. foreign investments now earn an annual return in dividends, fees and royalties of more than sixteen percent, a good part of which flows into the black-ink side of the balance of payments ledger. Far more importantly, in terms of jobs for Americans, export orders flow back to these shores from the overseas subsidiaries of U.S.-based MNCs. About forty percent of the total exports of multinational corporations consisted of such intracompany transactions in 1970, the latest year for which data are available. Those exports mean U.S. jobs.

Pfizer Inc., the pharmaceutical manufacturers, rolled up an astonishing corporate "trade balance" during the booming 1960s. Over the decade 1960-71, almost ninety percent of Pfizer's exports went to subsidiaries overseas while production abroad by Pfizer for import into the U.S. was only 2.7 percent of total sales by foreign subsidiaries.

As this example reveals, most of the production of overseas plants is for consumption within foreign markets, mainly in the country where the goods are manufactured. An American MNC subsidiary in France produces (mostly) goods for sale in France. The Pfizer Frenchmen know the French territory. In Pfizer's instance, the sale of American pharmaceutical products—made by foreign workers and sold overseas to foreign doctors by foreign "detail men"—reflects a giant stride forward in human health and well-being. But the U.S.-based MNC drug companies can't simply export pills; they must create whole foreign manufacturing and marketing systems. For example, Pfizer finds foreign governments, quite properly, as concerned with the health of their citizens as our own Food and Drug Administration: "In the manufacture and distribution of pharmaceuticals, a maze of local drug regulations on safety, efficacy, dosage forms, and labeling in other countries would make it extremely difficult, or impossible, for Pfizer to depend solely on exports from the United States," says a company statement.

In many instances, there is no other practical way for U.S.-based international firms to serve these markets. For example, it is competitively impossible to ship empty cans (which are ninety-five percent air) long distances. Can-makers must be close to can-users. The same holds true for other forms of packaging.

So it is that the Continental Group has equity interests in thirty packaging companies in twenty-three countries. Continental's chairman Robert S. Hatfield declares: "Worldwide packaging is a $50 billion business and it is on the verge of massive growth outside of the United States."

This statement applies with equal force to other U.S. industries as well. For example, that old American standby, Wrigley chewing gum, now finds its fastest growing and most profitable market is outside the U.S. in nations where chewing gum is a novelty, and just beginning a growth curve that occurred in the U.S. many years ago. "The whole chewing gum market overseas has been growing by leaps and bounds," a Wrigley executive exclaims.

What does increasing overseas consumption of such items as pills, tin cans and chewing gum reflect? The exciting reality of a rising standard of living. Precisely because the U.S. enjoys the highest living standard in the world, many areas of our domestic market tend to be "mature" or semisaturated. But most of the people on earth do not begin to live as well as most Americans, and they want to live better and longer. If they are willing to work harder for a better way of life, we certainly ought to be ready to rent them at least some of the ingredients—including capital and technology. That helps create the prosperous, peaceful and stable world we all want. It is also profitable for the importing nation, the exporting nation and the MNC. Is it really plausible to suggest that we can sit behind walls on a vast pile of capital and technology while people are starving and sick—and still say we want a peaceful world?

American multinational corporations must pursue high growth and high profit opportunities overseas in order to maintain the vitality of the U.S.-based corporate parents. For example, an executive of the Continental Group notes that the company's international operations contributed more to earnings than any of the individual domestic operations in 1973. International earnings, he says, "helped us to continue a high level of domestic capital spending for expansion and retooling—a level that would have been difficult to sustain on the basis of domestic profits alone." So, union leaders must think that through, too: overseas profits often provide the capital which is invested to create jobs here.

There is a great irony in the labor union complaints about job export and foreign investment. The irony is that their complaints are essentially a function of success. What success? The success of America's rebuilding a war shattered world; of Point Four; of the Marshall Plan; of a humane occupation of Japan and its democratization. That success, based largely on international commerce, has built a world more prosperous than men could have imagined a generation ago. That prosperity has washed across America, making labor union members able to own cars, and second cars, private homes, televisions, camper trailers, motorboats, and able, too, to send their kids to college. One of the fruits of that success is that prosperity has washed across other countries—able, energetic nations in Europe and Asia. We have helped build them up into equals. Now we have to compete with them under the rules of as fair and open a system of international trade as has ever existed, a system that helped create that tidal wave of prosperity. We can, of course, destroy that system if we choose. Or we can play within the rules, in a tough game, and still do very, very well in a world of coequals.

One economic world is a reality. The single, planetary marketplace exists. The idea whose time arrived a generation ago, one world, one market, is encapsuled in the multinational corporation. It is a uniquely effective means to all manner of human, national and international ends; it is uniquely capable of expanding human freedom while national development plans are realized and new international ties are forged. It creates the economic reality of human progress and well-being to which politics, sooner or later, must respond.

Those of us in the international business community are very proud of our record. More so than most, we are creating a better world.

I know this sounds preachy. Sometimes, when my wife and grown-up kids give me a hard time about the difference between what big business preaches and what it practices, I feel uneasy about the future of private enterprise. Public relations is not our strong suit. We never seem to be able to describe the creativity, the wizardry, and the inherent humanism of a dynamic free enterprise system. If we had to depend solely on some of the loudest defenders of "free enterprise"—particularly those on corporate payrolls—we'd be in bigger trouble. They too often end up being for private profits—and socialized losses via government bail-outs. That's too bad.

Fortunately, it's results that count. We believe in the free enterprise system because it delivers on its promises. Today, multinationals are a key part of that system. And that's why the rest of the world buys what the multinationals have to sell.

4.

A Labor Leader

That was very eloquent, Mr. Businessman. Very stirring. And by no means all wrong.

The labor movement in the United States is not anti-business, or anti-big business. In fact, we sort of like big business. Working people, through their unions, can exert much greater bargaining power on General Electric—threatening to close down 228 plants and tie up $12 billion in corporate assets—than could ever be exerted on Mr. Smith's Widget Factory, composed of a dozen workers laboring in Smith's expanded garage. And unlike some of our colleagues in, say, the European labor movement, we are not anti-capitalists who oppose "free enterprise." The American system of enterprise, based on economic rewards for creativity, for innovation, for efficiency, has generally served this nation well. Working in concert with an equally creative, innovative and efficient labor force, we have achieved a standard of living here, for workers, that has never been matched.

Our complaints with industry over the years have often been not against industry being too "free," but, in fact, with industry not being free enough, sometimes stifling competition and attempting to milk the government for subsidies that we all pay for. We have also attacked businessmen for a certain degree of hypocrisy: they are all for "freedom" for business to operate competitively, but are a little touchy about labor unions having the same sort of freedom to participate in the economic competition. The freedom for labor to strike for higher wages is as much a part of the free enterprise system as is the freedom for business to close an economically inefficient plant. Yet, business leaders over the years have been less than willing to accept that idea.

Still, as I said, we in the American trade union movement are not anti-business, and, in fact, as will be seen, we are not even anti-multinational. After all, we wouldn't be representing the Sheet Metal Workers Union if we said that Anaconda can't mine copper wherever the copper is—in Zaire, Chile, New Guinea, wherever. So, if our colleagues in the business community are under scathing attack these days, and if some, or much, of that attack is either misleading or trivial, then I for one am prepared to say so. And if, as we have just seen in the previous chapter, businessmen feel it necessary to fill the air with paeans of praise directed at themselves, we will not object. We have ourselves been the target of the same sort of mindless criticism. We understand the need to periodically pound one's chest and restate first principles.

But, having said that, I would also say that we are not going to be conned into giving either business or the MNCs a free pass. Because within this generally sound structure of free enterprise and free trade, there are some inordinately stupid things going on. They are so stupid, they threaten most of the things that Americans, and American businessmen, really want. These include: a healthy domestic American economy, a climate of freedom around the world and the continuation of the free market ethic.

One should begin by separating the component parts of the international economic picture: trade on the one hand, and direct investment on the other. Businessmen don't like such separations, but we trade unionists know from practical bargaining experience that taking apart a package deal is critical to an understanding of the problem.

Trade involves the flow of goods across borders. When that trade is truly "free" and truly "fair," when Uncle Sam doesn't get mistaken for Uncle Sugar (which happens all too often), the labor movement supports foreign trade. As was pointed out correctly, such trade can create American jobs.

But direct investment involves capital outlays to create jobs and factories outside the U.S. And the obvious fact of the matter is that foreign investment by American corporations is not generally, on its face, an automatically healthy thing for the American economy.

It is certainly not automatically healthy for that sector of the American economy called "working people."

The reasons are plain, and are generally acknowledged by many impartial professional economists. First and foremost: generally speaking a dollar invested at home is better than a dollar invested abroad. It's that simple. Why so? An American dollar invested abroad ultimately and principally helps the American economy in one way: it generates a flow of profits that sooner or later find their way back to America.

But a dollar invested in America also earns a profit. Now, that rate of profit might not be as high as can be generated overseas—which is why so many corporations continue to opt for direct foreign investment. Capital flows toward the highest return just as water seeks its own level.

The dollar invested at home, however, does more than just earn a return for its owner. It builds a factory in Kanawha or Multnomah. It builds an office building in Houston. It drills for oil on the North Slope. And as it does that, of course, it creates jobs for American construction workers, engineers, architects, factory workers and janitors. And it creates jobs for the Americans who service those people—shoe salesmen, and shoe factory workers, doctors and nurses, used car salesmen and so on.

Moreover, the dollar sent abroad doesn't directly help the American economy until after a start-up period, perhaps a few years. Then, hopefully, it begins to earn a profit, and then only some of that profit is remitted home. Now, after a few years, suppose that overseas dollar starts earning, say, fifteen percent after taxes. Suppose three-fifths of that profit, nine percent, is sent home (the balance is reinvested in Germany or Nigeria or Taiwan or wherever). At nine percent a year it would take eleven years to get that dollar back into our economy—plus, say, two years until the dollar even began earning a profit at all. Thirteen years for full repatriation! Thirteen years when much of that dollar is creating German jobs, or French jobs—and not American jobs.

That is the crux of the matter: the dollar invested here spreads 100 percent of its magic here, from day one of investment. Even before it becomes profit-making, it is job-making. Not so overseas.

But our complaining, the complaint of the labor movement, goes even further than that. The dollar at work overseas pays taxes overseas. Properly so. Money invested in a French factory ought to pay French real estate taxes. But money invested in America pays American taxes. Money invested in a factory in Canton, Ohio pays real estate taxes in Canton, Ohio. From the point of view of the corporate accountant, it doesn't make much difference if the taxes are paid to France or to the U.S. and to their citizens. But a tax dollar paid by a corporation in the U.S. may pay for a cruise missile, or cancer research, or crop subsidies, or dredging a nine-foot channel on the Ouachita River. If that corporation has invested its money in France, the missing taxes must be paid by the rest of us Americans, many of us dues-paying members in American unions. That loss to the Treasury of the United States must be paid for by the members of a Local of the International Brotherhood of Electrical Workers, who may be underemployed anyhow because General Electric decided to invest in a new plant in Brazil. A two-time loser.

There is at least one other potent reason why capital at home is better than capital abroad. It is a reason that we labor leaders do not forget. It was expressed very well by Lord Keynes some years ago:

> Consider two investments, the one at home and the other abroad, with equal risks of repudiation or confiscation or legislation restricting profit. It is a matter of indifference to the individual investor which he selects. But the nation as a whole retains in the one case the object of the investment and the fruits of it; whilst in the other case both are lost. If a loan to improve South American capital is repudiated, we have nothing. If a popular housing loan is repudiated, we as a nation still have the houses. If the Grand Trunk Railway of Canada fails its shareholders by reason of legal restriction or rates changeable or for any other cause, we have nothing. If the Underground System of London fails its shareholders, Londoners still have the Underground System.

What Keynes said is elementary. Capitalism is risky for the capitalist. He may lose his shirt in Burma or England. If he loses his shirt in Burma, then England has nothing to show for it. If he loses his shirt in England, the English may well have plenty to show for it—like his shirt.

Which leads us, quite properly, to England. For centuries, in fact even today, the idea of investment abroad has tantalized the English. It is an idea that has, in fact, been worshipped. That a small island nation with few resources could send its wealth to vast continents with no horizons dazzled British entrepreneurs. After all, they reasoned, the pounds sent abroad would generate a higher return than if they stayed at home. That higher return, they said, would come back to England and Englishmen would prosper. This view became particularly strong in the years from 1890 until the beginning of World War I, in 1914. During that time direct investment overseas went from £25 million a year to £200 million a year, an eight-fold increase! Incredibly, by the end of that period somewhere between eighty percent and ninety percent of British capital formation was being sent overseas!

It did not work out well, and Britons (although faced with many other plagues today) are still paying for their economic folly. It made some capitalists rich, but it also meant that industry at home was starved. There was no money for new plants and equipment, consequently no major increases in productivity, and therefore, no major increase in real wages, little decent housing and a sideways and even downhill economic spiral, the results of which are still being felt.

Luckily, it's not that bad in the United States—but it is getting worse. We in the trade union movement monitor the data carefully. In the period from 1967 to 1970, about sixteen percent of the capital invested by U.S. companies was invested in foreign lands. By 1974 that figure had climbed to nearly twenty-three percent. The comparable numbers for manufacturing facilities are even higher: twenty-one percent in the late 1960s, rising to thirty-one percent by 1974. Since then, the trend-line has remained fairly stable. What this means is clear: At a time when U.S. businessmen were crying about inadequate capital formation, massive quantities of American capital, somewhere between a fifth and a third of all our capital, depending on how it was measured, was leaving America.

We are not as foolhardy as the British were in the early years of this century, but the trend is the same. And it is not an accidental trend. Professor Robert Gilpin of Princeton, in his book *U.S. Power and the Multi-National Corporation,* points out that the movement of capital away from the world's dominant economy is a recurring pattern. The dominant economy, he says, becomes dominant by its ingenuity, resources, dynamism and general creativity at home. For a period of time, this bubbling economy not only bubbles at home, but it is also helped by the export of its unique entrepreneurial creativity. New methods of production and distribution are absorbed by other nations; the capitalists in the dominant economy sense large profits are to be made by exploiting this proprietary know-how through investment in the less sophisticated economies.

And in that tendency, Gilpin maintains, the dominant economy sows the seeds of its own decline. This movement of capital from the core economy to the peripheral economies has happened in many nations, most obviously and most recently England and the United States. For a certain period, it has been good for the dominant nation—expanding markets, increasing efficiency—but not indefinitely. In the U.S., says Gilpin, the point of diminishing returns was probably reached around 1960. Now, he says, direct foreign investment is a drain on the American economy, and unless checked and modified, it will drain away our economic vitality.

Gilpin's point is a good one. It seems to us particularly relevant these days because of the special nature of the technology that is being transferred along with the capital. It is no secret that there has been an explosion of technological innovation since the end of World War II. New drugs, computers, jet aircraft, lasers, automation, semiconductors have been developed, at staggering costs, largely in the United States. Much of these costs of technological development have been borne either directly or indirectly by the American consumer, including our union members.

How so? First, a great deal of new American technology was developed under government contract. The jet aircraft, of course, was developed by the Department of Defense. The military technology ultimately gave birth to civilian aircraft. Drugs are developed by private pharmaceutical companies, but much of the medical knowledge upon which the drugs are based has been developed through multi-billion dollar investments by the National Institutes of Health. It was the space program that helped develop Teflon and solid state circuitry, and provided the technology for the development of computerized banking and studless snow tires. All those technologies and scores more were paid for, in whole or in part, by the taxpayers' dollars.

And even the "private" research and development came from the American consumers, so many of whom are our comrades in the trade union movement. During the years when the remarkable American drug companies were creating steroids (e.g., cortisone) and supersophisticated antibiotics (e.g., tetracycline), these companies were not losing money. So their cost of research and development was being subsidized by higher prices on the drugs that they were selling here at home.

After all that cost has been borne by the American consumer, what does industry go out and do? It licenses the technology to foreign manufacturers at a fraction of the apportioned cost of development (after all, the technology now exists). Or the entrepreneurs build a plant overseas to use that technology at the same subsidized cut-rates. In either instance, the foreign market gets the free ride on what the American consumer bought and paid for.

That's unfair. It is also unwise, and in economics that's probably worse than being unfair. The massive transfer of technology is something very different from normal international trade. Structurally, it often stands with a foot in three camps: international trade, direct investment—and a third notion as well.

Consider this: If you sell a potato, or a pair of pajamas, or a bicycle, or sulphuric acid to a customer overseas, then after a relatively short period of time the potato, pajamas, bicycle or sulphuric acid is used up. But if you sell a modern steel plant or an automobile plant you are not exporting goods that are shortly consumed, you are exporting the means of production. Now, this may be a simple sale: no direct investment, not even any royalty or license fee. It is a sale of a "turn-key" factory, a complete modern factory with automated equipment, in much the same way as one would sell a single machine, or a pair of pajamas. Technically, it is called "international trade," but these factories, using sleek new technology developed at the expense of the American taxpayer soon start producing American-style goods, just as a "direct investment" would. These goods can be produced somewhat cheaper overseas because foreign workers, particularly in the less developed lands, earn less money than American workers and work under conditions that Americans wouldn't tolerate.

And what happens? First, some of these goods are sold back in the United States. The workers, our workers, who would have manufactured these goods are thrown out of work with all the attendant human and economic misery that that implies. But something else happens as well. The goods produced in those newly economic, newly efficient foreign plants are exported to markets in third countries, cutting into American exports that would have filled those orders. And the result of that is still further American job loss. We lose every way. We cut our domestic market and our foreign market!

What we are doing in the name of free enterprise is a little crazy! The English exported capital, it's true. But at least they made great efforts to keep a lid on the export of their then unique technology. Remember, that was one of the great complaints of those thirteen colonies—that they weren't even allowed to develop their own manufacturing industries!

So, there is something wrong with the multinational system from a macroeconomic view. And something wrong with its one-way technology transfer.

And, thirdly, there is something wrong with it from the point of view of simple morality—at least as we trade unionists see it.

For at least forty years, labor in America has been fighting, and winning, some bruising battles. We fought for the right to bargain collectively, we fought for the minimum wage and Social Security (as earlier we had fought to stamp out the abuses of child labor), we fought for vacations and pensions, we fought for occupational health and safety, we fought for environmental protection.

We won all those fights. And now what happens? Those great multinational benefactors come to our working man and say, "Congratulations, you've won your battles; you've now got everything you wanted! Except for one thing: you don't have a job anymore. We're closing down the factory."

What makes that happen? One thing is that the American's job will soon be performed by a fourteen-year-old girl in Taiwan using new American-designed equipment. But that girl has no labor union rights, she works in an unsafe plant and she has no pension or vacation benefits. The factory is not subject to environmental laws. It is, in fact, part of what is now called a "pollution haven."

What do we Americans do then? We salve our conscience. We say, "Don't worry, Mr. Worker. After all, the government will help you. They'll retrain you. You're only fifty-five years old. That's the prime of life. You're lucky to get out of working in a shoe factory. Unskilled work. How would you like to be a computer programmer? You can move from Needham, Massachusetts to Lubbock, Texas to get a new job. There's a very big demand for fifty-five-year-old inexperienced computer programmers in Lubbock during a stagflation. Then, Mr. Worker, you can come back to Needham once a year for Christmas and visit your grandchildren. You can see how much they grow from year to year.

I must say, we regard that as immoral.

And there is something more, while we're talking about immorality. American businessmen are eloquent about the free enterprise system. We just heard some of that eloquence. Open markets. Open competition. Free flow of capital. To hear them tell it sometimes, it's like a religion.

Listen, do you know who our workers are competing with today? Not with other American workers at the Acme Widget Factory, which also has a union. They are competing with teenagers in Taipei. Soon, if current trends continue, they will be competing with Ivan, in Lenigrad, whose boss is the state. The Soviet state not only doesn't care about unions or free enterprise or free markets or labor mobility or a free press, or free emigration, it also publicly acknowledges that it is actively pursuing a global policy of expanding the hegemony of those Leninist precepts justifying economic slavery. And I use the term "slavery" advisedly. (You may read all about it in the text of Brezhnev's speech to the Party Congress.)

There is a great irony about this. All these up-to-date Fortune-500 corporations have "forward planning" groups. They fly around the country going to conferences about the likely shape of the future. They will figure out to the last decimal place the market for copper cathode in 1993, or the demographic structure of Lesotho in 1997. But when it comes to things that really matter to them, when it comes to things that they have some influence over—like whether freedom will survive on this planet, for themselves, for corporations and for their own children—about that their forward planning extends to about the tips of their noses!

So we really have one big question: Is anyone up there paying any attention? In the name of phony free trade, are we creating deep, irreparable and harmful shifts in the nature of the American commercial and industrial landscape? Is multinational direct investment an automatic good thing?

Is anyone in this government even asking such questions on a case-by-case basis? Is anyone looking and asking questions not from the business point of view, not even from labor's point of view, but from America's point of view?

Take the case of "manufacturing." Now, that sector only involves about twenty-five percent of America's annual GNP. And it is there that the great change has occurred in multinational development. No one quarrels with the idea that oil companies have to go where the oil is. That is a red herring raised by the Businessman. But manufacturing? Why should manufacturing enterprise be exported? Is that good for America? Is anyone in government really asking that question?

In 1958, America's portion of total world exports of manufactured goods was twenty-seven percent. By 1971 it was nineteen percent. And the most recent figures from 1978 show that figure now to be only fourteen percent. That trend first manifested itself in the simpler, more labor-intensive sorts of industries in America.

In the fifteen years from 1956 to 1971 there was an absolute loss of jobs in manufacturing industries and much of it due to direct American investment overseas: 50,000 jobs in women's apparel, 20,000 in shoe manufacture.

But it wasn't just low-wage, labor-intensive industries that went overseas. In the same period there was a drop of 109,000 jobs in electronics. From 1957 to 1971, as steel imports climbed, about 100,000 job opportunities in the American steel industry were never realized. Other high technology capital-intensive industries showed losses: 45,000 in nonelectronic machinery, 75,000 in electric equipment—all from 1966 to 1972.

By 1972, imports (often financed by direct U.S. investment) made up seventeen percent of steel sales, twenty-three percent of auto sales, twenty-five percent of women's apparel, thirty-five percent of shoes, sixty percent of sewing machines, sixty-one percent of phonographs, sixty-four percent of black and white TVs and ninety percent of radios and tape recorders.

Even that's not all of it. Not long ago McDonnell Douglas licensed the Japanese firm of Mitsubishi to build ninety-one copies of the F-4 Phantom jet fighter. We didn't sell the planes; we sold the ability to make planes! Is all this really in America's best interest?

The business philosophy is that it must be good because it conforms to Adam Smith's sacred doctrine of comparative advantage. But as far as Labor is concerned, comparative advantage is dead. It is based on two assumptions, which in the last fifth of the twentieth century are simply invalid. First, there is no free trade; the U.S. is a semifree trade island in a protectionist world. Second, the "advantages" that Adam Smith talked about are mostly gone, the victims, ironically, of multinational machination. It's true America has special advantages. We have capital. We've got management techniques. And we've got merchandising know-how. To name a few.

And the American multinational corporation has grown rich by exporting all of those special advantages. We send our money overseas, with it goes our technology; with that goes our managers and engineers and advertising people. Accordingly, foreign factories now have the same "advantage" plus other "advantages" like low wage rates and protectionist [1] economies.

We maintain that this pattern of the exodus of manufacturing industries is not good.

In 1973 we caught a glimpse of the future. The oil states got together and turned off our oil. And suddenly, commuters in Denver couldn't get to work, and farmers in Marshalltown, Iowa couldn't fertilize their fields.

We drew exactly the wrong conclusion from all of that. We clucked, "Well, we live in an interdependent world." What we should have said is, never again. That means that we must retain (as much as possible) the ability to control our own destiny. The definition of that is not interdependence. It's independence.

We give lip service to it. Nixon ballyhooed Project Independence and now we import almost half of our oil, substantially more than at the time of the 1973 oil embargo. We're potentially more vulnerable to OPEC now than we were then. Are we going to let Saudi Arabia call the shots for America?

Listen to Professor Gilpin:

> Foreign investment was the *easy* way, the easy way for corporate expansion, the easy way to get energy. Instead of spending money on energy research, instead of looking for ways to use coal, we invested in Arabian oil wells. It was profitable while it lasted. But the party is over. We have overemphasized foreign investment, to the detriment of the development of our own domestic resources and opportunities, especially in terms of energy.

What have we learned from the energy situation? Apparently nothing. We blithely encourage the export of our nation's invaluable manufacturing capability. Mind what I say: we not only allow that capability to go overseas (even that might not make sense) but we encourage it. We give tax deferrals. We give tax credits for foreign tax payments, but only tax deductions for tax payments to state or city governments in America. We insure firms against expropriation by foreign governments. We encourage, via Item 807, the assembly of component parts for American products in Mexico. We have our commercial attachés in U.S. embassies around the world serving as errand boys for American multinationals. And the loser is the manufacturing sector.

Don't get me wrong. Our creative businessmen would be delighted to export our agricultural wealth too—if they could figure out how to ship out the flatlands of the Middle West. They'd take over the service economy, too, if they could get an American to go to Mexico in order to get a haircut or watch a ballgame.

But manufacturing capability can be exported. And it is. And no one up there asks: "Is this good for America?" The businessmen say it doesn't matter. A job lost in manufacturing will be picked up in the service economy. It will be picked up, they say, because profits coming back from overseas investments will be used by shareholders to buy swimming pools for their suburban homes thereby triggering domestic employment. The man who builds the swimming pool will then buy his lunch at Roy Rogers, employing a high school kid as a counterman. It's an old business argument: feed the horses to feed the sparrows.

Does all that make sense for America? Do we really want a fast-food economy? Do we really believe that other nations in the world, under the lash of nationalism, will endlessly keep remitting profits back to the "Yankee imperialists?"

We have already felt the sting of an oil embargo and the hostage taking of revolutionary Iran. Do we want to be even more under foreign control? The more we invest in foreign lands, the more vulnerable we are to foreign pressure. Excess foreign investment is the economic equivalent of heroin. We have become economic junkies: the only protection we have of our foreign investment is the promise of more foreign investment, a bigger fix, otherwise the host country will mistreat investment that's already there.

Do we want to be viewed as the white-collar nation that earns its way off the sweat of others, clipping coupons to the tune of a modern-day *Rule Britannia*? Are we prepared to say that a modern economy can exist with all superstructure (service) and no foundation (manufacturing)? And what happens to the American workers and pensioners whose future well-being depends on the economic viability of companies that have been systematically starved of capital for modernization?

The United States is, and can remain, one of the most self-sufficient nations in the world. Or we can sell off our self-sufficiency. We can succumb to, instead of combatting, the notion of interdependence. The solution, of course, is not either/or. Not either autarchy or interdependence. But both. Encourage a solid base of self-sufficiency. And encourage a free flow of trade and capital when it doesn't erode our own economic, political or military security.

But is anyone in this government seriously and systematically asking and acting on these questions? The Carter team made a half-hearted analysis of the impact on trade with the Soviet Union—and promptly even forgot about that. But, no one in this government looks at the big, historical picture.

We have created something called GATT (General Agreement on

Trade and Tariff). It does an imperfect job at regulating trade in the world. Our negotiators consider imports, item by item, of every classification of trade.

Why don't we have a GATT for direct investment?

Time is running out.

NOTE

1. There is yet another irony. We actually encourage foreign protectionism by our multinational investment. How? Well, the Businessman said it in the last chapter: When foreigners won't let our goods in (i.e., are protectionist) we reward them by investing there to beat their protectionism. So we reward *their* protectionism with *our* free-flow of capital. Terrific! (Yet, we have no counterpart policy to force foreign investment here.)

5.

A Foreign Policy Activist

Because I am nonpartisan in this debate, I shall begin by stating categorically to both the Businessman and the Labor Leader as follows: you each have a good point.

Because I am an American, and a deeply concerned one in this era, I have come to this view: the fact that there is so much to be said on either side of the multinational question should be used to America's advantage. For, the real issue is not profits or jobs; the issue is freedom and national security in an unfree, unsafe world.

Let me explain by stating some first principles and building my edifice brick by brick. First, what is the goal of American foreign policy? There are many goals, of course. Peace is surely number one. As he left office in early 1969, Dean Rusk was asked to name the proudest accomplishment of his eight year tenure. "We kept the genie in the box," he said. And he was right. Our first foreign policy goal is a negative one: to avoid arguments that get settled in the shadow of mushroom clouds. Immediately behind that goal is another negative one: to avoid "limited" wars. In the vernacular that translates to "No more Vietnams."

But that is all obvious. If that's all there was to it, ours would be an easy task indeed. What we seek is not just peace. We seek a certain kind of peace. Simply put, we seek a peace where that intangible called "the American way of life" can survive and flourish.

No problem, you may say. We have nuclear overkill and therefore deterrence through "mutual assured destruction." The Russians aren't going to attack us. Nor will they land amphibious forces in San Francisco or Nantucket.

Not so simple, I'm sorry to say. For two generations, American foreign policy architects have acted on the premise that freedom in America is not likely to survive as an isolated phenomenon on this globe. If the world is, say, half-free, our Western notion of freedom and human dignity probably can survive as a flawed blessing we may pass along to our posterity. But if the world is, say, ninety percent unfree, can America survive in such a world? Not likely, say our best thinkers. And I agree.

So we have a role to play, in our own self-interest, to see to it that freedom and the hope of freedom survive elsewhere. This, of course, is the stated goal of President Carter's "human rights" policy, to encourage freedom to flourish. Now, that goal is not easy to achieve. There are powerful, potentially expansionist, hostile forces in the world, sincerely committed to diminishing what they regard as the dangerous blight of excessive freedom. Accordingly, we are required to make and meet commitments with allies who share our values.

This has been our strategy for thirty years since the end of World War II. From Japan and Australia to Turkey and England, we almost single-handedly stitched together all the "freedom-loving" nations in the world into a common economic, military and diplomatic enterprise. Our tools in forging this great freedom alliance were the elementary ones: we strengthened our allies by pouring billions of dollars of aid and investment into their economic infrastructure, we formed common military links and we pursued joint diplomatic strategies. And soon, we had created the most far-flung, powerful and prosperous alliance in the world's history.

Now, according to many observers, much has changed. Our collective military strength is no longer superior to that of the Soviet Union and its Warsaw Pact satellites. In fact, many military experts assert we either are "number two" or will become "number two" unless we change our policy and our priorities. As our military power wanes, some of our diplomatic links have become more fragile. Many observers believe that the grand alliance suffered as

Americans slogged through Southeast Asia, and the case is made that it suffers today as the Middle East simmers, as Greece and Turkey feud, as Iran crumbles, Afghanistan succumbs and Cubans serving as Russian Ghurkas roam across Africa. The idea of "freedom" is still paid lip service, but the new and less developed nations of the world shun its practice.

One need not accept as gospel every example of alleged deterioration (and there may well be some scare-mongering going on) in order to feel a certain clammy political sensation. It was symptomatic of the general retreat of American power when Dr. Kissinger noted these developments, and others, and suddenly began quoting Spengler's *Decline of the West*.

It is my strong belief that there is nothing fated and inevitable about that gloomy, Teutonic prophecy of a half century ago, and nothing preordained about America's perceived drift toward inferiority and isolation today.

What to do? Two obvious answers:

- *Strengthen our military forces.* Fine. But they will never regain the clearly dominant position that they had in the fifties and early sixties.

- *Re-weave the fabric of our diplomacy.* Fine; we should try to do it, and can expect to achieve some success. But, it too cannot be as it was a decade or two ago.

What to do? Our cause remains the survival of freedom, but our military and diplomatic power are declining, at least in relation to the recent past. Clearly, we must look toward other means to bolster our strength and insure the survival of our commitments and of the values we hold dear.

What to do? Examine clearly the use of our economic power as an instrument of national security and survival. Consider the wealth weapon.

Let me begin by telling you what I think about multinational corporations. I happen to believe that American multinational corporations are useful entities—not only economically but ideologically. As one who believes that the survival of freedom in the world is the key issue, I regard the following as one of the central facts of our time: There is not a single *noncapitalist* democracy in the world today. Capitalism, we have learned, is an economic system under which freedom may flourish. It doesn't always, but it may. That has not yet been demonstrated by socialist states, the so-called people's democracies.

So I'm for capitalism, and for its instrumentalities, like the multinationals. As it happens, they are one of the means through which much of the so-called "American way of life," the democratic way of life, is disseminated around the world. (And I'm not talking about the corruption scandals.)

Hundreds of thousands of Americans are employed all around the globe by MNCs. In many ways—not in all ways, but in many ways—they are exemplars of what America stands for. They are responsive to consumers, as the businessman noted. They are technology-oriented. They are efficiency-oriented and production-oriented. And, yes, they are also profit-oriented. If there are ideas more necessary in this world, particularly the less-developed world, than responsiveness, efficiency, production and profit—I'd like to know what they are.

Our people come into a country as part of ABC, Inc., and they bring in capital and technology and marketing skill and put it all to work. Sometimes the investment is toward a rather modest end— how important, after all, is a bubble-gum factory in Brazil? But, for the most part, the business goals also serve socially useful ends. They mine copper and drill for oil; they build bridges and roads; they manufacture consumer goods and set up chains of retail shops. They do it in ways that have often not been previously seen or understood in the host country. Moreover, the ways in which these things happen, happen to be the ways that are critical to the process of modernization and Westernization.

They do these things better than anyone else and I happen to believe that Americans do these things better than anyone else because of the nature of our society and the nature of our culture, which happens to be free, entrepreneurial and open.

So I am pro-multinational in some deep and profound ways. Please remember that as you follow the rest of my argument: it comes, believe it or not, from an ardent free enterprise pro-capitalist.

Call my position cultural imperialism if you must, or economic jingoism, but whatever its name, it reflects a basic fact of international life. And that is this: on the level of commerce and popular culture, the globe is being Americanized. On the level of geopolitical conflict, unfortunately, the tide may be running the other way.

That geopolitical conflict is not as simple or clear-cut as we once thought it was. But, it still has something to do with fundamentally differing ideas about (a) the role of the state in man's daily life, and (b) what social and economic system can best make poor people into not-poor people.

The successful resolution of this conflict is at the heart of our foreign policy, because it will determine whether a free America survives in a climate of world freedom over the next several generations. In that struggle those efficient, innovative giants called multinational corporations can be effective allies in carrying out a constructive American foreign policy. How?

The discussion in the preceding chapters has shown one thing clearly: nothing is very clear. The businessman says that multinational enterprise and investment overseas is just wonderful for the American economy. The labor leader says the opposite. One says imports are necessary and wonderful; the other has doubts. Is it possible that the truth lies somewhere in between? In fact, isn't it even probable that the truth in this instance is to be found in grey-shaded areas? And if that is so, isn't it likely that that is a fact that can be exploited?

We are one of the most self-sufficient nations in the world, and we can be quite a bit more independent indeed if we choose to be. If some aspects of international trade were curtailed, that too would not be a disaster. (Only seven percent of our GNP is derived from international trade, compared with, for example, eighteen percent for all other OECD nations.)

Therefore, if we choose to somewhat reduce foreign investment or trade, it will not hurt us; not much, anyway—in the short run it might even help us a little. Unlike many other nations, it is a course we can at least publicly and credibly consider.

That this is so gives the United States enormous flexibility in the use of our economic potency to achieve national political goals in the international arena. We can flex our muscles without harming ourselves in any significant way. Remember that. It is a key to my argument.

And yet, we haven't used this inherent economic flexibility. Why not? Why have recent administrations been so blind to the potential political influence inherent in our economic wealth?

I'll tell you one reason why. Because to some extent they were under the influence of rigid, doctrinaire big-business Republican ideology.

And, I'll give you a second reason why. Because the current movers and shakers in the Democratic party are so scarred by Vietnam, they are afraid of international muscle-flexing, even non-military muscle-flexing (i.e., the wealth weapon). Let us examine, in turn, each of these self-defeating philosophies.

The Republican party, as presently organized, is so imprisoned in the big-business ideology that it refuses to see America's economic potency as a true instrument of national policy. Too many Republicans are obsessed with the specter of "more government regulation." They have an irrational fear of "tampering with the marketplace." Because of their paranoia, they refuse to see that playing economic hardball may be a useful, sometimes absolutely necessary means of preserving and protecting our way of life. Many of the same businessmen who rallied 'round the flag during World War II and won the production battle on the home front under government leadership refuse to see any similar role for government today in the contest with the Soviet Union or other U.S. adversaries. The business community and its political handmaidens may well have put themselves in the ironic position of sacrificing free enterprise on the altar of free enterprise.

Harsh, you think? Well, maybe a bit harsh. But, it's a nice phrase—and there is a root of truth there. The liberal Democrats, on the one hand, are not terribly upset about government regulation. But, they have become enslaved by another Republican doctrine: détente. You'd think Nixon and Kissinger had been Democrats! The code phrase for the limp-wristed wing of the Democratic party is: No Linkage. (Unfortunately, the Limp-Wrists seem to dominate the Carter foreign policy apparatus.) Why no linkage, particularly, on economic issues? Because it upsets the Russians and if you do that you might renew the Cold War. What these Democrats fail to understand is that détente—a strategy designed to end the Cold War—may have turned out to be a strategy that is losing the Cold War. As an afterthought, these same liberals don't want to ever upset the Third Worlders, because those poor fellows have been oppressed and are therefore morally superior. The fact is that the liberals are always frightened. They have lost their nerve!

Let me give you a series of examples. You will notice they are mostly examples of things we haven't done that we might have done. Why haven't we done them? Because they conflict with either the boilerplate ideology of big business, an ideology that even many in big business no longer believe in, or the boilerplate of détente ideology (Don't Rattle the Russians!) that most voters find repellent.

Consider oil. More specifically, consider one aspect of a terribly complicated situation in which there are no good guys, and much confusion. Consider the pathetic American response to OPEC's blackmail.

In 1973, the OPEC countries, acting as a producer cartel, quadrupled oil prices. In 1979, the OPECs did it again—a 75 percent price hike. We are paying the price for these extortions. They have been partly responsible for double-digit inflation, one steep recession and the growing possibility of another. They are directly responsible for the stagflation still afflicting the world economy. And we are now more vulnerable than ever to another oil boycott.

Now there are ways to try to break a cartel. Through inaction, stupidity, short-sighted political pressures, and because of free enterprise rigidity, America has done exactly nothing to break up OPEC. On the contrary, we have seemed to appease and protect it.

One way to deal with a producer cartel is to set up a buyer cartel. An international buyer cartel would be best, but in this instance even a U.S.-only buyer cartel would be more useful than doing nothing.

It might work something like this: The U.S. imports about 6 million barrels of oil each day. It is purchased by thousands of brokers, commission agents, small companies, medium sized companies and some super big companies. In a classical free market, these buyers could shop around for the lowest price of oil, and in the process of this shopping around, they would keep the price of oil low, particularly in times of a "glut." But, if a producer cartel imposes a single price system, there is not very much that the thousands of American buyers can do to nudge prices down (particularly because our antitrust laws discourage such collusion between companies). So the producers slap their cartel prices on every barrel and, with a little shaving here and there, that price sticks.

But, suppose America set up a Petroleum Buying Board, as Harvard economist M. A. Adelman and others have proposed. Under that sort of plan, only the U.S. government could purchase and import foreign oil for those thousands of private free enterprise companies. There would be only one buyer for 7 million barrels of oil per day, sold under sealed bid to encourage producers to secretly undercut one another.

What could such a Supreme Oil Buyer do? It could pay a call

upon the producers of oil in certain small-to-medium sized nations around the world where we do some business—say, Ecuador or Nigeria or Indonesia. Call that nation Indocuageria.

We could go to the Indocuagerians and say to them, as follows:

> Dear Friends: We are buying a good deal of your oil. We are paying you twenty-odd dollars a barrel. That money keeps your country afloat. You realize $10 billion a year from our purchases, even though your entire production capacity is not being used. We wish you well. But we also wish us well. We do not want to pay twenty-odd dollars a barrel. But we'll buy every drop of oil you'll produce, in time of oil scarcity or oil glut. You will realize about $15 billion a year from this: a lower price per barrel but you can vastly increase production, increasing gross revenues. Your nation will prosper and flourish. On the other hand, if you do not sell us oil at $15 a barrel, we will buy none of your oil, your nation will go into an economic tailspin and the political opposition will see to it that General Glotz, your esteemed President, will probably be looking for a new line of work, if, in fact, he is lucky enough to stay out of the slammer and lucky enough not to meet with a traffic accident.

That is one way to break or at least bend a cartel when the oil situation is in glut status, as it periodically is (early 1978, for example). Somewhere around this globe there is an oil-producing nation willing to accept an offer that cannot be refused. But such a Godfather-like offer cannot be made by any one company, no matter how large, and particularly not by a company that is involved in production and marketing on behalf of OPEC members.

There are, of course, many other political strategies designed to erode the OPEC cartel. Many are listed in a 1979 *Harper's* article by Craig Karpel, "Ten Ways to Break OPEC." Mr. Karpel's suggestions are many, varied and culled from many sources. Some ideas make a great deal of sense, some less so but almost all involve the action of *government* in an active muscular manner, using our wealth as an instrumentality of power—a wealth weapon. But, so far, our government rejects using tough-guy and cartel-like tactics against OPEC, which is able to use these methods with impunity against the U.S. and other oil consumers.

Although the U.S. imposed import quotas in the 1950s and 1960s to keep out "cheap" foreign oil and protect Texas producers from price-cutting, we refuse to apply the same kind of government activity and intervention to break the grip of the cartel. One reason such a policy is rejected is that it is said to be incompatible with free enterprise. Another is that it might offend the sensibilities of Third Worlders. I say OPEC is incompatible with free enterprise. More important, it is incompatible with a national instinct for survival not to examine such measures.

Let me give you another example of how the mindless, reflexively pro-business mentality deprives the United States from pursuing certain policy initiatives.

It is in America's best interests that basic human liberties in the Soviet Union be expanded.

Why? Here is a short version of a long answer. We want to, uh, "relax tensions" between the U.S. and the U.S.S.R. That's what détente was all about. What are the causes of those tensions? Many things. Superpower rivalries. Nuclear weapons. Conventional armed strength. An American view that the Soviets tend toward both adventurism and expansionism if left unchecked. And the closed nature of Soviet society.

Why that? What interest do we have in the national condition of Soviet society? The answer can be determined by sensing what the situation might be if the Soviet Union had a society modeled, say, on England. Or Israel. Or Sweden. All socialist or semi-socialist nations, but free nations. Would we be as concerned with potential Soviet expansionism if what was expanding was Swedish-style socialism with Swedish-style civil liberties? Of course not. We might not like it, but we wouldn't be saying that the possibility of Soviet expansion would undermine and endanger the Western notion of freedom.

We are bound to resist potential Soviet expansion because of the nature of the U.S.S.R.'s system and its brutal assault on humanity. As Milovan Djilas, the Yugoslav dissident, has written: "It is a life and society to all intents and purposes ordered . . . into a kind of total violent madness. . . . The regime as a whole (is) unreal in its derangement and real in its force and deception."

If this is one cause of tension, it is equally true that such tensions would be relaxed overnight if the Soviet government were to allow greater civil freedoms within its borders. We would have less to fear. That is one reason why the U.S. and other Western nations insisted that the Helsinki agreement have a "third basket" of accords that dealt with human freedoms. But, significantly, that basket of agreements was violated by the Soviets before the ink was dry. It was seen as a total mockery by the whole world at the time of the Scharansky trials. Any expression of individual liberty is seen as a threat by the comparatively tiny elite who exercise total control over the Soviet population and exert a somewhat weaker and less direct grip over the subject populations of Eastern Europe. The old men of the Politburo are a frozen gerontocracy who dare not ease up, dare not yield to consumer desires and dare not cease their military buildup for fear they will be overthrown.

There is, in addition, another set of reasons that provide a rationale for America's interest in "the internal affairs" of its pre-eminent adversary. According to data provided by high-ranking Soviet defectors and confirmed by our intelligence analysts, as much as sixty percent of the U.S.S.R.'s total industrial capacity may be devoted to military and defense production! That kind of war mobilization leads to war-risking adventurism. Wouldn't an increase in human and political freedom in the Soviet Union tend to encourage some economic freedoms that might encourage the shift of Soviet productive resources to peaceful purposes? In democratic countries or semidemocratic countries, after all, consumers exert a powerful directive force over the goals of the national economy. And they don't order up increasingly powerful rockets with nuclear warheads.

In the recent past, the U.S. has acted on the idea that actively encouraging liberalization in the U.S.S.R. is in America's best interests. In March 1973, Senator Henry Jackson introduced an amendment to the trade bill that provided that the United States would deny "Most Favored Nation" (MFN) status to any "non-market" country that did not allow free emigration. Although widely construed to be a measure designed to help foster the emigration of persecuted Jews from the Soviet Union, the Jackson Amendment actually dealt with all emigration from all nonmarket nations. Presumably, it would also apply to Cuba, Vietnam and other unfree countries seeking to trade with America.

The strategy behind the Jackson Amendment was straightforward. The Soviets wanted to be in a position to increase trade with the United States. They wanted access to our energy-producing and industrial technology. To help pay for that, they needed a favor: the reduction of anti-Iron Curtain discriminatory tariffs and the bestowal of "Most Favored Nation" tariff status—a status which is almost automatically granted to any non-Iron Curtain nation.

Jackson's amendment linked MFN to emigration from the U.S.S.R. He noted that the right to free emigration was the quintessential humanitarian safeguard and, in fact, was guaranteed by the United Nations Declaration of Human Rights, of which the Soviet

Union is a signatory. Jackson said: Live up to that international agreement and you get MFN. Don't—and you don't.

Ultimately, an amendment to the Jackson Amendment sponsored by Senator Adlai Stevenson also linked the granting of large Export-Import Bank credits to the Soviet relaxation of emigration restrictions. These credits, extended by an American government bank (the Ex-Im Bank), are considered essential by American multinational corporations seeking to make big deals with the Soviet Union. (The bank extends credit to the Soviets who use the funds to pay the corporations and then repay the bank over the years.)

Thus the linkage was made: we want an expansion of freedom, you want expanded trade with the U.S.—*let's swap*. You get what you want; we get what we want.

Critics maintained that the Soviets would never go along with the deal. It was, they said, an intolerable interference in their internal affairs, as though the Soviets never, never interfered in any other nation's internal affairs. Secretary Kissinger said that the way to gain concessions from the Russians was to whisper privately in their ears; any attempt at a public arrangement would fail.

But the Russians did go along with the deal. Representatives of Senator Jackson and Secretary Kissinger met over a period of nine months hammering out a detailed series of specific arrangements to define exactly what would represent compliance and/or good faith on the part of the Russians. Secretary Kissinger negotiated for the Russians, and checked every comma and semicolon with them while negotiating with Jackson over the content of the agreement. On October 18, 1974, at the White House, Jackson and Kissinger met with President Ford to release the contents of a series of letters that spelled out the arrangement.

Six weeks went by. Senator Stevenson and Senator Harry Byrd added further amendments to the trade bill linking the Ex-Im credits as well as MFN to liberalized emigration. The Russians then suddenly attacked the proposal, revealing denunciatory letters written six weeks earlier.

And Kissinger and Ford, heavily supported by the business community, denounced Jackson, not the Russians! The Jackson Amendment, they said, echoing the Soviets, interfered with Soviet internal policy. The Soviets couldn't be expected to change their policy just for some trade advantages, however important.

The mysterious question remains: Did Kissinger lie or did the Soviets? Was Kissinger, as he indicated, clearing the terms of the deal with the Soviets? If he was, why did the Soviets change their minds and denounce what they had agreed to? And why did Kissinger and Ford (and most of the business community) apologize for the Soviets, attempting to turn an American wealth weapon into a wealth boomerang?

Did wealth weaponry work? Did the Jackson Amendment work? Did it push the Soviets into relaxing emigration standards? The latest emigration data show that the Soviets want trade more than they want to restrict emigration. They are beginning to respond because we hung tough. Should it be continued? There are many answers. Kissinger didn't like it. Vance doesn't like it. Businessmen don't like it; it makes trade difficult. Some liberals don't like it; it upsets our partners in détente. But a man closer to the scene does like it: Andrei Sakharov. And I like it. Someday maybe we'll see just how effective it, and legislation like it, really can be. That day will come when our presidents and secretaries of state support "linkage" instead of undercutting it.

The list goes on and on. In early 1976 two big items were on the bargaining table between the Soviet Union and the United States.

One concerned a massive sale of American grain to Russia. Not for the first time, and not for the last, the Marxist economic paradise was unable to feed its people and came hat in hand to the running dogs of capitalism to seek help.

At the same time that the Russians wanted grain they also wanted Angola. Accordingly, they dispatched massive amounts of armaments to their guerrilla clients there and sanctioned the use of Cuban mercenaries in the fighting. (The Soviet Union subsidizes the Cuban economy at the rate of at least $3 billion per year; when the Russians whistle, the Cubans heel.) Yet, no one in the White House suggested publicly to the Russians that they should stop subsidizing the export of revolution and use the money to grow more and more wheat and feed grains. Or that we Americans would refuse to allow the Russians to have their world revolution and their grain, too.

Those of us who believe that economic power is a plausible tool in international politics had a simple plan. Tell the Soviets they can have one, not both. Get the grain—don't get Angola. Take Angola—don't get the grain. It was pointed out that if the tables were turned, if America was making an expansionist move and at the same time was relying on the Russians to extricate us from a tough domestic situation, they surely wouldn't let us have both.

But the Ford administration rejected that tough-minded course of action. The grain, they said, was being sold by private companies. Our farmers had been told to plant fence-row to fence-row. Any restraint on grain support would interfere with private enterprise and depress the price of wheat. (An election was coming up.)

Of course, there are ways to deal with those problems. Licenses to sell to the Russians can be revoked. Farmers' wheat output in excess of domestic and normal export needs can be bought by the government at world prices and held in storage. An embargo can be imposed. In the recent past, the U.S. has, in fact, slapped an embargo on soybean exports, which stunned our close ally, Japan. But, then, we have treated allies like enemies and enemies like friends in recent years.

Alas, we are told, those tactics would violate the sacred free market. You might have to set up a government wheat buying board (copying the arrangement in that terrible unfree country of Canada). It would interfere with the giant grain companies' ability to do business around the world (trading secretly with the Soviet government and telling Washington nothing). It would lead, we are told, to socialism, or worse. Besides, such economic hardball might upset the Soviets and upset détente—heavens forfend!

So, the Russians got the grain. They also got Angola. And representatives of the private grain companies secretly negotiated in Moscow without any guidance or "interference" from our government.

Actually, we lost twice in those negotiations. We also said that we wanted to barter the grain for Soviet oil, in a half-hearted attempt to reduce the world price of oil. The Russians didn't like that; it might get them in trouble with the Third Worlders. So they refused and we just sold them the grain anyway, without getting a drop of oil. Meanwhile, the Cubans overran Angola. Such are the fruits of "détente." Small wonder that Ford and Kissinger were strung along the campaign trail in 1976 with the line that détente had turned into "a one-way street."

Another thought: America produces as much grain for export as does the rest of the world put together. The U.S. is the Saudi Arabia of grain production. We are the Faisals of food. Our secretaries of agriculture have frequently talked about "agri-power" and how useful it can be, should be and may be to the U.S. But somehow none of them ever recommends that we actually use agri-power.

In the United Nations there are scores of nations, mostly impoverished, that make a practice of excoriating the United States. We are, they say, racists, imperialists, resource gluttons and robber barons, responsible for all the world's ills. Moreover, they consistently vote against American interests on a wide variety of questions.

That, of course, is their privilege. But is it our duty to feed them?

Whenever the suggestion is made to tie our agricultural might, or any economic linkage, to our professed political goals, three basic complaints are heard. One is on humanitarian grounds, and that is fair enough. We don't want to be responsible for people starving to death, nor would we be. The second, ho-hum, is that the use of agri-power would interfere with the operation of the free market. That, of course, could not be tolerated. We have too much government regulation already, as everyone agrees. And the third is that Third Worlders should never be bullied, shoved, nudged or tickled in any standard political manner. Victims of a colonial past, of which Americans are surely partly guilty, the poor fellows now deserve a free pass. (It was so unbecoming of then U.N. Ambassador Moynihan to treat them like sovereign equals!)

Most of these instances have their roots in the Nixon and Ford administrations. But the Carter folks are no better, I fear. Their blue-ribbon National Security Council task force, headed by Dr. Samuel Huntington, had all the right ideas. Not just sticks (Dulles), not just carrots (Kissinger), but each of them as appropriate. They isolated the Soviet's vulnerable point: the need for oil technology. They put the oil technology on the "controlled list." And then what happened? Do you have to ask? The incredible Big Business-Left Wing coalition swung into action. Encourage trade! Dump the Jackson Amendment! said the American businessmen in Moscow in late 1978, lobbying their own government while Secretary of Treasury Michael Blumenthal and Secretary of Commerce Juanita Kreps stood by smiling with their Russian hosts. Back in the State Department the détentists swung into action: Don't stir up the Bear! they said. Withholding U.S. oil technology might sour the Soviets on SALT. And what happened? The Commerce Department started approving a steady stream of technology transfers to the U.S.S.R. And the Soviets, during the same time, continued a massive arms build-up, took over the government of Afghanistan, helped subvert the government of Iran, put MIGs in Cuba capable of carrying offensive nuclear weapons to U.S. targets—and so on and so forth. No linkage allowed!

Now, let's be fair. All of these issues are complicated. In each instance there is a rebuttal case to be made. Moreover, past experience has demonstrated that economic weapons, when wielded as a blunt instrument (embargos, for example), are usually worse than useless. But could we use economic power more skillfully and intelligently, as a scalpel?

Perhaps we can. Remarkably, even Dr. Kissinger, now that he's a civilian again, seems to agree. Indeed, he now seems to favor the concerted use of the very same weapon he opposed when Jackson proposed it.

In a speech on June 28, 1977, Kissinger said we need:

> . . . a unified strategy on the part of the industrial democracies (in dealing with the Soviet bloc). When the restraint of one becomes the windfall of another, it encourages not Communist responsibility but a strategy that divides the industrial democracies and uses their shortsighted obsession with immediate gains to undermine their long-term security. For years, there was an intense debate in the United States about extending credits to the Soviet Union, which were never planned to exceed $1 billion and would have been tied to specific projects and conditions of international restraint. Within two years of the enactment of the Stevenson and Jackson amendments, other industrial democracies had expended open-ended credits exceeding $10 billion. The need for a conscious and deliberate strategy among the industrial democracies for East-West trade will become ever more urgent as the scale of East-West trade grows.

Wealth weaponry. And the need that Dr. Kissinger talks about will remain unmet, I predict, as long as the U.S. fails to assert leadership with our own businessmen and our allies. The Carter administration, pledged to admirable human rights goals, had the golden opportunity to forge an economic alliance designed to meet major political goals. This administration, on its face, was less encumbered by the political constraints of big business boilerplate. Beneath the surface, however, it was peopled by former members of the Trilateral Commission, a pro-big business, pro-trade-with-Russia organization. And beneath that surface was the peace-at-any-price left-wing of the Democratic party. The Carterites were ruled by the same economic myopia that undermined the Nixon and Ford foreign policies.

I have cited specific instances of American failure in the past: OPEC, Jackson Amendment, Angola, agri-power, oil technology. But what of the future? What general ideas might be forged into a policy scalpel?

There are many such ideas. Of course, not all would prove feasible. But all should be investigated. Carefully. With an open mind. In fact, a few mini-steps have been made, which should be noted.

Shortly after then-Ambassador Daniel P. Moynihan rocked the United Nations in early 1976 by telling the truth in broad daylight, the United States announced that the U.N. voting records of all nations would be regularly scrutinized and, in fact, tabulated by computer. Those nations that consistently voted against America's interests would thereafter likely find it difficult to remain on the State Department's list of recommended recipients of foreign aid. Of course, such an arrangement doesn't interfere with free enterprise because the aid is given, not sold, and so, under a Republican administration, the program was initiated, representing a small but promising step toward political realism.

There is no evidence, unfortunately, to suggest that any follow-through occurred in the Carter administration. Their policy is "don't be beastly to the Third World,"—with no exception.

Just as we don't like repression of the human spirit in leftist totalitarian countries, so we do not like repression in rightist totalitarian countries. Actually, these days we are, and should be, somewhat more tolerant of repression on the right than on the left for two reasons. First, the rightists don't usually have the established, far-reaching statist bureaucracy and police apparatus of the totalitarian left dictatorships. Second, and most important, no right-wing totalitarianism or coalition of right-wing totalitarianisms has 2,250 nuclear-tipped intercontinental ballistic missiles pointed at America.

Still, we don't like repression anywhere, and it is in our national interest to help end it, as President Carter rightly declares. This is so if for no other reason than to gain enhanced moral credibility for our truly self-interested effort to ease repression in the Soviet bloc.

Of the recent right-wing dictatorships in the world, probably none has been harsher than the government of General Augusto Pinochet in the once-flourishing Western democracy of Chile. When the Pinochet government took over from Allende's crypto-Communist government in 1973, mass arrests, deportations, torture and other violations of civil liberties ensued. For several years, Chile remained under tight military control which the Pinochet regime said was necessary to keep the nation from backsliding into Communism.

In April 1976, William Simon, the secretary of the treasury and no left-wing counter-culturist, journeyed to Chile and, as they say in the political trade, sent them a message. We understand, he told them, that you have been through a lot. Communist subversion and a near-takeover, incredible 1,000 percent inflation, social dissolution. We understand your fears, and the reasons for your hardline domestic policies. But, it's got to stop, or start stopping, if you want any further help from Uncle Sam. If you want our loans, our credits, our corporate investments, our diplomatic support give us a sign. And then keep the signs coming.

Before Simon's visit to Chile ended, fifty political prisoners were released with great fanfare. The week after he left, another fifty were released. A trickle of signs turned into a freshet, giving rise to hope that the Pinochet regime had permanently relaxed its grip on Chile and begun to restore freedom. What the Republicans started in Chile, the Democrats intensified. In this instance, at least, the Carter administration has kept the heat on the Santiago government by criticizing violations of human rights and holding up aid grants.

In mid-July 1977, President Pinochet took Chile and the world by surprise by announcing a two-stage plan to restore democratic government, with presidential elections possible by 1984. Soon afterward, Pinochet announced the disbanding of the secret police.

If Chile rehumanizes, there will be bipartisan credit enough to share between Democrats and Republicans. They used U.S. moral influence and economic power for important political objectives—ironically, the equivalent of the Jackson Amendment with a Latin beat.

These were small, halting, specific steps—and some were abandoned. But Chile is a small country that offers no major threat to the U.S. There are bigger fish to fry, if we resolve to get back in the fish-frying business.

Neither Democratic nor Republican administrations have covered themselves with glory in dealing with the whales of the world. The human rights language in the 1976 Democratic platform attacked the Republicans for not using the human rights issue to advantage vis-à-vis the Soviet Union. The subsequent Carter human rights policy started out with a tough posture toward the Soviets, the one nation in the world that is a potential threat to the U.S., has an abominable human rights policy, and seeks to export their views. Alas, the Soviets didn't like it when we pointed out their shortcomings. So President Carter stopped the rhetoric, and undermined any action to link our economics with their politics. A policy designed to deal with strong adversaries soon turned into a policy to harass weak allies! Too bad. A great opportunity was lost.

The question before us, then, is still a general one: Should we, and can we use America's productive power in a continuing way to help achieve our aims in the world? Such a general question needs some general answers and principles, and then a few specific proposals.

First, if we agree that we should seek to use our economic potency in the political arena, let us vow not to kill the goose that lays golden eggs. We wish to harness that goose. Our motto should be drawn from the Hippocratic Oath: "Do no harm." We do not want to harm MNCs. We appreciate the creative economic energies they have unleashed. We admire their efficiency and their innovativeness. Now, we'd like to get them to help pull the sled.

Second, let us have further disclosure of the costs, prices and taxes of multinational corporations. We cannot use our economic potency if we are kept in the dark about how the machinery works. Information is now too sketchy.

Third, neutralize the tax code. Not only my friend the labor leader, but other informed observers believe that aspects of our tax policy are skewed. This is so, they believe, because of tax laws enacted during the early post-World War II era—laws designed to encourage U.S. overseas investment. These analysts believe that it is often more profitable because of artificial incentives for a corporation to invest overseas rather than in the U.S.[1] Insofar as they are correct, the tax code ought to be neutralized. This is important for several reasons: (a) to encourage the truly free movement of capital according to the organic laws of the marketplace; (b) because the original situation (the need to rebuild the war-torn economies of Europe) has passed; (c) it's fairer to American workers; and (d) from my own perch as a foreign policy tactician it will be much easier to use the policy "scalpel" effectively if foreign investment is not made artificially more attractive than domestic investment.

So much for ground rules. Beyond them are certain specifics that should be carefully examined. I am not an economist, but I will suggest here some items that seem to make good sense and that ought to be considered by the economists of the Carter administration. They will serve not as a comprehensive list, but perhaps as a set of pointers toward an eventual policy.

Elimination and Selective Reinstatement of Tax Deferral. The tax code now allows a MNC to forgo bringing back overseas profits to the United States, and to forgo paying U.S. taxes on that money until, or unless, that profit is brought home. This, of course, encourages MNCs to re-invest foreign profits in foreign lands. It is a privilege not permitted these same corporations in the United States. The rationale for it: to put the overseas subsidiaries of U.S. companies on an equal competitive footing, in terms of relative tax burden, with other companies operating in the same country.

Nevertheless, tax deferral is a favor. It is a favor to host countries because it provides incentives for U.S. foreign direct investment. It is a favor to U.S. corporations because it gives them an opportunity to avoid certain taxes and use the money to create new assets and new cash flows.

Now, the key question: Since when do we give away favors? And particularly, since when do we give away favors to other nations? Typically, nations trade favors. So perhaps we might use tax deferral as a swapping device and not a free gift.

Here is one possibility: eliminate tax deferral, then selectively reinstate it to achieve political goals.[2] That would be a device that could be used in a variety of ways.

For example, if it was the United States' stated intention to provide more help for the nations of the Third World, we could reinstate the tax deferral privilege for any MNC investing capital in a less-developed country. That might lure some investment capital away from Western Europe (which already has a high standard of living) to Africa and Asia (which doesn't).

As a further refinement, we could reinstate deferral only in those less-developed countries that did not pursue actively anti-American policies. Or, we could give it to rich nations and poor nations alike just so long as they were not actively anti-American. Or, we could use this as a lever with our allies to see to it that trade policy toward the Eastern bloc is unified, preventing the Soviets from playing off one Western nation against another.

The possibilities are abundant, with but one caveat: any such policy tool must be handled like a scalpel, not like a buzz-saw. What this would do, frankly, is allow us, in a small way, to politicize some of our international economic activity. Perhaps I should not use that word; it is generally considered bad to politicize anything. Surely, if handled in a bumbling way, it could get us into trouble. But in a political world, it does give us a tool with which to protect our political as well as economic interests. Moreover, it is not such a radical new thought: after all, "Most Favored Nation" trade status has been granted, and withheld, on a political and ideological basis for decades.

Export Controls of Capital. Many nations, indeed most nations, have some form of government control over the flow of investment capital to foreign lands. For a variety of reasons, this would not be easy for the U.S., not in a world seemingly awash in dollars already exported. Yet my labor friend asks for a "GATT for investment." If by that he means a steady monitoring of dollars that are still flowing from the U.S., I think it is an idea that is worthy of examination. Such outwardly-bound dollars should be looked at from the point of view of both the domestic job situation and the world political situation. It would add to our arsenal of carrots and sticks.

Export Control of Technology. This is the "know-how" capital that will create wealth for generations to come. Japan, an ardent champion of free trade in goods, does not practice free trade in high technology such as advanced semiconductors and very large integrated circuits. The blend of politics, economics and technology behind the latest drive of "Japan, Inc." is worth studying because it has great, if not immediately apparent, relevance to the concept of "the wealth weapon."

Semiconductors are as basic to modern industry today as steel was two generations ago, a fact the Japanese government clearly understands. As developing countries catch up with Japan in producing steel, automobiles and consumer electronics, and as markets become saturated with these products, Japanese planners are striving to leap ahead, and largescale semiconductors offer a springboard. The director of electronics policy of Japan's powerful Ministry of International Trade and Industry (MITI) says, "The computer industry is the future money-earner in Japan."

In the early 1970s, MITI reorganized the Japanese computer industry, combining six major companies in three development ventures. Over the next five years, the government provided $225 million in research and development subsidies to hasten the arrival of a new generation of Japanese computers. These companies signed cross-licensing agreements giving them complete access to the technology of their American competitors. However, and this is critical, apparently the advanced technology derived from work sponsored by the Japanese government will not be shared with outsiders. In contrast, in the U.S. the results of government-sponsored work that can be patented enter the public domain. Uncle Sugar? Maybe.

U.S. manufacturers of semiconductors, watching Japanese production capacity mounting beyond domestic needs, are worried about a future surge of exports to the American market. They claim the U.S. television industry waited too long to react to Japanese government-assisted import competition, and was overrun as a result. "We believe in free trade," said a founding member of the newly created Semiconductor Industry Association, "but free trade with ground rules." This is not a classical free trade outlook, but a prudent one in the contemporary international political economy. Our government should heed it.

If the aim of such ground rules is to enforce trade reciprocity—in the case of semiconductors, a two-way flow of technology and equal competitive access to domestic markets—it might not be a bad idea for the U.S. government to have at least stand-by technology transfer controls as a bargaining tool. Their existence might be the best guarantee they would not have to be used.

If we can even consider using such a tool in our bilateral economic relations with so close and friendly a trading partner as Japan, we should certainly not recoil at the prospect of using similar bargaining tactics in our dealings with the Soviet Union and the Eastern bloc. A "GATT for technology," admittedly difficult to establish or enforce, could provide us with still more carrots and sticks, for use with allies and adversaries in different ways.

Export Promotion Techniques. Naturally, if we create disincentives, we should also create, in much greater abundance, positive and potentially profitable incentives to business for expansion of exports in politically desirable areas, attuned to national interests and goals. Tax-based incentives would be most effective.

Zero-Based Access to our Market. As the Jackson Amendment strategy noted, our most potent economic asset is our market. No nation on this globe can get wealthy or stay wealthy without access to the incredible buying power of the 225 million consumers in this consumer common market we call the United States.

Acknowledging this, we ought to consider the leverage it gives us. To begin with, how about zero-based quotas? We allow certain products—beef, textiles, specialty steels—into the U.S. on a quota-per-country basis. These quotas have come to be regarded as God-given rights by their recipients and each year there are attempts to raise the various quotas from their perceived God-given floors. How about starting from ground zero each year? It's our market they want access to—and that's another set of carrots and sticks that we have but don't use.

And what about nonquota products? Only when things reach a catastrophic level, as with television sets in 1977, do we demand an Orderly Market Agreement (OMA), restricting imports. How about zero-basing that procedure and examining the barn door before the horse has left? Again: more carrots, more sticks, all available to help gain our various foreign policy objectives. After all, if we use OMAs to protect American workers against external economic forces, why not use OMAs to protect all Americans against external political forces?

This all may sound very prolabor, I know. But do not delude yourself, Mr. Labor Leader. These same principles can be used to reward our friends as well as make life difficult for adversaries, or raise certain quotas to help our friends. It may mean increasing foreign investment, increasing imports according to a coherent plan. Wealth weaponry involves carrots and sticks, and labor will have to show its statesmanship when it's carrot time.

You get the idea. Let us consider the development of new economic tools to promote our national self-interest and indeed our survival. It is not likely that all of these would work out. It might take years to phase in others in a nondisruptive manner.

But at the least we should try to construct a coherent and integrated politico-economic system. Economic "adhocracy" is a luxury we may not be able to afford if we want to preserve the sort of world where economic freedom, and other freedoms, will survive and flourish.

At the least, we should use our economic leverage to demand that our allies pursue a unified policy toward granting credits toward freedom's adversaries. That much is critical.

This process, constructing an integrated politico-economic system, will be the ultimate test of the vision of the Carter administration. The tools are available—agri-power, cartel-breaking mechanisms, deferral policies, zero-basing and, undoubtedly, scores of other devices. The key question is: Is the will also present?

It has been said that when economics becomes important enough, it becomes political. International business is now important enough to the future of the United States that its conduct has become a form of international politics and should be subject to sympathetic guidance, but guidance nonetheless, in the national interest.

I would maintain that in the long run such an approach, coolly thought out and moderately implemented, would not only be in the long-range best interests of America, but also in the long-range best interests of the business community.

Businessmen tend to think only in terms of making the world safe for profits. The policy I advocate would help make the world safe for freedom—the only system that allows profit.

NOTES

1. It is not only the tax code: a federal agency called OPIC (Overseas Private Investment Corporation) insures U.S. companies against foreign takeover, thereby encouraging overseas investment. But shouldn't this be a normal business risk? Why should the U.S. government help our businesses invest in nations that might want to destroy them?

   Professor Raymond Vernon, Director of the Center for International Affairs, Harvard University, and the leading U.S. authority on multinational corporations recently declared: "On the whole, I am inclined to think that the period has passed in which OPIC can clearly be justified in terms of U.S. national objectives and even of global welfare." In 1976, Senate investigators found forty-one percent of the insurance written by OPIC went to just eleven multinational corporations.

2. As a variant, tax deferral could be eliminated just for new investment with a grandfather clause in effect for investment already in place.

6.

A Third World Leader

I must confess that I have listened to the preceding discussion with mounting anger and disgust. If I harbored any doubt about the justice of my position, your completely unfeeling words have resolved them.

All of you talk of having opposing interests and positions, but you are brothers under your well-scrubbed pink skins and well-fed bellies. Capitalists, so-called labor leaders, activists, academics, liberals and conservatives—Communists, too—all of you see and think about the world in the same way. You have only one common interest: the perpetuation of the global system of exploitation that supports your outrageous privileges.

Gentlemen, you are all on the same side, and I am proud to be on the other. You are on the side of greed, gluttony and oppression, and I am on the side of humanity—the winning side.

I've listened to the businessman make a pretty speech about unifying the world through economics. By that he means the same old world in which businessmen and their henchmen run everything and the rich get richer and the poor poorer. In my kind of world, the rich must transfer wealth to the poor, not as charity, but as matter of right.

Our labor union friend doesn't represent real "workers"—he represents petty bourgeois consumers who want more money and more comfort at the expense of those overseas who have nothing.

As for the so-called foreign policy activist, he is a joke. He wants to manipulate the poor as though we are puppets without thoughts or desires of our own. He babbles on about freedom, never understanding the central fact of our time: hungry people aren't free. A full belly is more important than a free press.

President Julius Nyerere of Tanzania has spoken our deepest desire: "The poor of the world must demand a change, in the same way as the proletariat demanded change in the past."

We of the hungry, cheated developing world, the Third World, are not only asking you to create a "New International Economic Order." We are demanding it. And we are doing everything that we can to bring it into existence. With or without your assistance.

In truth, ever since OPEC succeeded in lifting the price of petroleum to a just level, the new economic order has begun to emerge. The rise of OPEC is the most revolutionary development of our time. It is at once the precondition for, and the prime mover of, the long overdue shift of power and wealth away from the tiny rich minority and to the deprived majority among mankind.

The four-fold increase of petroleum prices was much more than an economic act. It was an act of political liberation. It was not done out of selfish motives for the exclusive benefit of the members of OPEC alone. Quite to the contrary, OPEC acted for the benefit of the entire developing world to dignify the terms of international trade. It acted to revalue the primary commodities of the nations of the Third World, promote their long-term economic development, and, most important, open up the only peaceful path to the future—the path of full equality among nations. OPEC is causing the world's wealth to be redistributed for the benefit of the producers, and this is the essential precondition for peace.

OPEC's historic example has proved the success of using countervailing power, resources versus industry, to correct international injustices. It has fired the imagination of the Third World and enabled us to see political and economic reality in an entirely fresh way. We no longer see ourselves as weak. We are no longer resigned to having decisions intimately affecting our lives made in the remote inner circles of the West, by the anonymous masters of the giant multinational corporations. Now we see our vital interests clearly and demand that we shall decide how these are to be served. The recent events in Iran only underscore the fact that the tide is turning. Iran is now its own master—finally!—and the multinational businessmen have retreated with their tails between their legs!

Accordingly, we shall set commodity prices—and at fair levels. We shall control the unimagined mineral wealth on the floor of the sea. We will see our debts renegotiated. We will see preferential tariffs for our goods.

The industrialized countries of the northern hemisphere persist in seeing developing countries of the southern hemisphere as mere children engaged in a noisy rebellion. Therefore, the so-called North-South dialogue is largely an exercise in futility in which Henry Kissinger and other cynics have tried to buy us off with crumbs from the table of capitalism. But the cumulative impact of the OPEC price increases and other unilateral producers' adjustments in the world balance of power soon will overturn that table and force the industrialized countries, especially the United States, to change their outlook.

That will be the next stage of the global revolution of equality— the rise of a new social awareness and desire for social justice in the capitalist countries. They must realize that their own future well-being and perhaps their very survival depend on the sustained development of the poor nations, and that henceforth these nations must be dealt with as equals. "The urgent need," says Carlos Andres Perez, the president of Venezuela and an important spokesman for our revolution, "is to alter the economic collision course between North and South before the two great regions of our planet find themselves in open confrontation. This would surely have a negative effect on those of us in the Southern Hemisphere, but those in the North must ask themselves who has more to lose."

Americans ought to understand better than anyone else what is actually happening in the world economy because it is not so very different from what happened inside the United States two generations ago under the New Deal. Indeed, in an effort to remind Americans of their modern heritage and encourage them to apply its lessons, Mahhub ul Haq of Pakistan, the Harvard- and Yale-trained director of policy planning at the World Bank, makes the New Deal-New Economic Order analogy explicit in his book, *The Poverty Curtain: Choices for the Third World*.

Haq believes that the world is approaching the same point as the United States in the 1930s, "when the New Deal elevated the working classes to partners in development and accepted them as an essential part of the consuming society." He likens the poor nations to "an emerging trade union," which has the basic objective of negotiating "a new deal with the rich nations through the instrument of collective bargaining." What do the poor nations want?

Haq says we seek:

- *Greater equality of economic opportunity through the sharing of trade, production and investment.* For example, the developing countries now have only seven percent of world industry. Their share should rise to at least twenty-five percent by the year 2000.

- *"The right to sit as equals around the bargaining tables of the world," where decisions affecting the Third World are made.* As Algerian President Boumedienne declared: "The raw material producing nations insist on being masters in their own houses. Developing countries must take control over their natural resources. This implies nationalizing the exploitation of these resources and controlling the machinery governing their prices."

- *Redistribution not so much of past income and wealth—all of the Third World's current demands do not add up to one percent of the combined GNPs of the rich nations—but rather of future growth opportunities.* This would be accomplished by using the international counterparts of the domestic, post-New Deal "social mechanisms" such as welfare programs used to uplift the poor in the United States.

- *Acceptance of the new international economic order, not as the outcome of a single negotiation, but as an historical process extending over a long period.* The result would be a gradual but fundamental change in the world balance of power in favor of the poor nations, and their inhabitants who comprise the global majority.

Haq hopes, and so do I, that the industrial nations, led by the United States, will be wise and far-sighted enough to weigh the costs of disruption carefully and choose accommodation and cooperation over confrontation. The rich nations should recognize, he writes, that "any conceivable cost of a new deal will be a very small proportion of their future growth in an orderly cooperative framework." If the rich resist change, Haq declares, "the real bargaining power of the poor lies in their ability and their willingness to disrupt the lifestyles of the rich. In any such confrontation, the rich have far more to lose and are generally far more willing to come to a workable compromise."

I don't want to sound truculent or threatening. We in the Third World, after all, urgently need your assistance. But it must be extended on our terms, not on those imposed or won through bribery by your multinational corporations in the past. The scandalous revelations concerning the conduct of your big companies abroad—the payoffs, political interference and wholesale corruption—add up to a sordid chapter in the history of our time. It is also a closed chapter. The events in Iran have shown that Yankee must behave—or Yankee go home.

Sometimes I wonder whether some Western businessmen ever read a history book or even scan a newspaper. Many of them seem totally unaware of the forces that have reshaped the modern world and revolutionized men's thinking. By far the most powerful force is nationalism. Yet the executives of transnational corporations seem unable to understand or respect it. Perhaps because, with good reason, they no longer feel much pride in their own countries, they are insensitive to the strong, proud sense of national identity and independence in the Third World.

In any event, those who control so-called global corporations, which have headquarters but no real homes, must adjust to our way of thinking before we will allow them to do business in our countries. We will not permit them to reimpose piecemeal the colonial dependence and imperialist master-slave relationship of the past. These businessmen must accept a basic proposition: economic development shall be for the benefit of the majority of the host country's population, not for the rich minority or for the foreign corporation and its shareholders.

The chief purpose of economic development is to lift poor people out of their poverty. The singleminded pursuit of maximum profits and the emphasis on rapid economic growth for its own sake do not contribute to this noble human purpose. The endless, open-ended search for superaffluence is the suicidal madness of the West. But we reject it, and we oppose its invasion of our homelands.

Regardless whether the famous "Club of Rome" still endorses the conclusion, there are definite, clear-cut "limits to growth." We all know this to be true from our direct observations of life. A man cannot eat more than his fill, or cultivate all the land he sees, or catch every fish in the sea. He must limit his appetites to what he can productively use, or else his waste will in the end destroy his wealth and his health.

So it is with the multinational corporations that covet our national resources and wish to exploit our oil, minerals, and other commodities. They must be taught to curb their appetites. It is nothing short of criminal that the United States, with less than six percent of the world's population, consumes fully a third of the world's raw materials. Because so much of our natural wealth is nonrenewable, it should be used carefully, with an eye to the long future. Again, OPEC offers a splendid model. It has forced the oil-consuming nations to think about the immediate and long-term costs of using up petroleum, and about what must be done to provide energy alternatives before the oil runs out.

I have lived long enough among people in the Western industrial world to realize how impatient most of you are. For you, the only moment that seems to matter is now. People in the developing world are more patient because they have little choice. Their lives are not ruled by the gods of efficiency and productivity, and they are not slaves to the clock. They are also less reckless and wasteful with what resources they have precisely because they have so little. They have no margin for error, while you enjoy big, fat cushions against misfortune. We literally cannot afford to approach business the way you do, and we cannot allow you to impose your ways on us.

For example, you possess much advanced technology, which you transfer to our countries according to your engineering and economic criteria, not ours. You often send capital-using, labor-saving technology. It is very efficient and profitable, but it contributes nothing to our development because it does nothing to remedy the evils of massive unemployment and under-employment. You are preoccupied with cutting costs and increasing profits. We are worried about jobs. And in our countries, we demand that you worry about them, too.

The transfer of technology is a highly complex subject, and the international code of conduct now being negotiated is badly needed to establish clear rules. But the governing proposition can be stated simply: the transfer of knowledge, like the redistribution of wealth, is an obligation of the rich to the poor within the world community. The transfer must be chiefly for the benefit of the recipient. Otherwise, it is merely a disguised form of exploitation and colonization. Therefore, the terms of the transfer must strictly adhere to the needs of the recipient, as that nation defines them.

The test of whether the transfer is occurring on the basis of full equality is whether the recipient-nation is able to generate its own technology and thus achieve its own independent growth. To help the developing nations catch up, the advanced industrial nations, through their multinational corporations, should be required to give them preferential access to desirable technology. I repeat: this is a gift—we owe you nothing in return.

This requirement, founded on the obvious need for sharing to make equality a reality, goes to the heart of the concept of the New International Economic Order. In this emerging economic order, all nations shall become equal in fact only by treating some as more equal than others in practice for many years to come. Preferential treatment is a form of "deferred reparations" that the industrial nations owe the developing nations to compensate them for past injustices. For a generation or more, you shall be poorer so that we may be somewhat better-off, a small compensation for generations of injustice.

In the relations of Third World nations and multinational corporations, there are literally a host of questions to be resolved—everything from the elimination of their corrupt interference in our internal politics to the proper method of pricing intracompany transactions that are often used to cheat the host-country's tax collector. Yet all such questions, however complex and detailed, ultimately are questions of power.

The relationship between host developing country and multinational corporations rests on the power equation between them. In the past, it has been lopsided in favor of the corporation, which bought and bullied its position of unequal power. Now, it is our unalterable intention to tilt the factors in the equation decisively and permanently to the side of the developing country. And if you don't like it, *stay home!*

7.

Rebuttals

Authors' note: Now rhetoric and interests and facts collide head-on. Each participant in the discussion must defend his arguments and attempt to rebut the others. After hearing the indictment that has brought him to the dock of the court of world opinion, our friend from the business community began this discussion. The apparently simple rules of fairness would suggest that he speak last in this part of our round-robin. But that is not to be. Fair, maybe. Logical, no.

The businessman made a case, and made it well, we believe. That case was attacked, blunted, even savaged by three spokesmen with different perspectives: a labor leader, a foreign policy activist, and a Third World leader, in that order. The businessman must now have the opportunity to answer these attacks.

And, by similar logic, the labor leader shall go second. He had a chance to hear and deal with the businessman's argument, but not with the Third Worlder's views nor with the Activist's views. He'll get his chance here, and soon, and then he'll get a chance to rebut the businessman's rebuttal as well. So too, in order, will we hear from the spokesman of the developing world and from our friend the Activist.

When all the rebutting and counter-rebutting is concluded, the reader will have an opportunity—in Chapter Eight—to hear directly from the authors.

Businessman: Thank you, all. Everyone here seems agreed that MNCs are really quite effective instrumentalities for producing and distributing goods and services. That is in striking contrast to recent public rhetoric—and we businessmen are grateful for it.

There is only one small trouble with the specifics of what each of you recommend. If enacted, these proposals would clearly erode and perhaps even destroy that very relationship which you claim to respect. These proposals represent a direct attack on the goose that lays the golden eggs.

What none of you ever seem to understand, no matter how often we businessmen say it, is what it is that makes free enterprise so productive. The answer is the combination of incentive and freedom.

Every proposal I have heard strikes at the heart of those two essential concepts.

Consider the views of the labor leader. He says, plaintively, "No one up there is paying any attention." He says, "We're losing jobs" and quotes numbers that have been massaged, kneaded, bent and distorted beyond imagining. He says, "Let's have a GATT for MNCs, a case-by-case governmental review of each dollar invested abroad."

First of all, it should be pointed out that GATT in all its permutations from the Kennedy Round in 1961–62 to the recent Tokyo Round, has always had the goal of encouraging international commerce. Now, Big Labor wants a new-fangled GATT to discourage international investment.

The short-sightedness of the labor leader's view has become increasingly apparent. Suddenly the patterns of investment flows are changing. Substantial amounts of foreign money are coming to America, creating jobs in America. Is that bad, Mr. Labor Leader? These are union jobs, Mr. Labor Leader!

Let me repeat one precept: Denying business the ability to direct its capital freely toward targets of profit opportunity diminishes the ability of that business to provide whatever people want and need, wherever they need it, in the most efficient manner possible. It's as simple as that. Freedom yields efficiency and productivity. Controls erode efficiency and productivity.

Sure, if a government board had to approve every foreign direct investment on a case-by-case basis, that would curtail the flow of

American investment overseas. But what would happen to that capital?

Let's consider the case of Acme Widget Corporation. Acme Widget already has a large share of the U.S. market. Its major American competitors, the XYZ Widget Corporation and Metropolitan Widget Corporation, are also solid, aggressive firms, each with a substantial share of a market generally saturated in terms of widget usage.

Acme makes a net profit each year of $10 million after taxes. A generous $5 million is paid out in dividends to stockholders. Above and beyond depreciation, about $2 million is earmarked to keep the U.S. plants modernized and to build an addition to one plant. That leaves $3 million.

Acme had planned to invest the $3 million to build a new widget plant in Italy. Why? As it happens, Italy was near-virgin territory for widgets: like most MNCs, Acme goes overseas for markets, not cheap labor. Acme had been trying to sell made-in-U.S.A. widgets there for some time, but found that they were being undersold by local Italian companies and other non-American multinationals, that were already beginning to establish a beachhead in the attractive Italian market.

Acme figured it could earn about fifteen percent per year on its $3 million widget plan in Italy—about $450,000 coming back to the U.S. every year. In addition, some of the component parts of the widgets would still be manufactured in the U.S., creating additional U.S. jobs. Good for Acme. Good for U.S. workers. Good for Italy.

Now consider the impact of Big Labor's big idea. Here comes the National Council to Supervise the Allotment of Capital to Overseas Areas! And, after fourteen months of bureaucratic runaround, this all-wise Council decides that Acme Widget should not be permitted to export that $3 million of investment capital originally destined for Italy. Let Americans learn to consume more widgets, says the all-wise Council.

What to do? Several choices now face Acme. None of these choices is as beneficial as the company's original invest-in-Italy decision: not for Acme, not for America, not for Italy, not for the world at large.

Consider: One alternative course Acme can follow is to invest that $3 million in a new line of business. (Remember, the American widget market is near-saturated.) Acme can put the $3 million into a new line of carbon-paper-sets. That is a growth industry. The new all-wise Council on export capital, for one example, will surely encourage consumption of carbon paper at an enormous rate.

But Acme knows widgets, not carbon paper. In recent years, the American industrial landscape has been awash in a flood-tide of red ink generated by companies—"conglomerates"—that thought they could be a force in lines of business they know nothing about. Shoemaker, mind thy last! Acme, watch thy widgets!

Some of Acme's other choices to use the $3 million are (a) simply pay an even higher dividend, (b) invest the idle funds in "commercial paper" (the IOUs of other corporations) or Treasury securities, or (c) buy-in shares of its own stock on the market, which is shrinkage, the opposite of growth.

There are, however, some problems with such passive forms of investment: they produce below-par returns (in normal times about five to six percent versus fifteen percent or more in overseas investment) that trail behind the rate of inflation and, more importantly, they lead to a risk-avoiding nonentrepreneurial outlook that sees no particular reason for growth. Acme was once a feisty business, properly prepared to gamble on its ability to make a better widget and get a high return on its money. Now Acme, under government pressure, will become the next thing to a savings bank. And society suffers. If government can arbitrarily dictate where and how capital will be used, the incentives to risk-taking and innovation—to build a better mousetrap, to search for a new miracle drug, to design a computer the size of a telephone—are removed, and businesses stagnate. Society is denied the benefits of progress paid for by unfettered widget-making. If other countries imitate the U.S. and, similarly, keep their capital locked up at home, regardless of market opportunities elsewhere, it means the gradual end of economic risk-taking and a slow halt to progress throughout the industrial world.

The same basic flaw covers each argument advanced by the labor leader and by my other colleagues. To the degree that you deprive MNCs of economic incentives and freedom to operate, by that degree you ultimately deprive the people of the world (including especially the people of the United States) of the fruits of man's creativity.

Thus the labor leader rails against "technology transfer." But such transfer is a two-way street. Labor leaders surely want to keep the jet aircraft industry in America. But they forget that the original jet technology came from overseas. So did radar. And television. And tape recording. And the smaller Japanese motorcycles, whose proprietors are now building plants in America to help to turn out the one million units per year sold here. And some of the new "wonder drugs" that our slow-moving government bureaucrats deny us. Here is a fact that technology-transfer advocates had better consider: the growth of foreign patents is now greater than the growth of American patents! Do we want to exclude ourselves from that technology?

America is not the only innovative nation. And if we don't share what we discover with others, well then, others won't share their discoveries with us. The basic argument for both free trade and freedom of direct investment involves the breaking down of walls. Labor's argument ultimately leads to erecting walls. Every nation would have to have its own expertise on everything. Even the United States can't completely go it alone anymore, as witness our mounting oil imports. Are we really ready to endorse a policy—in the nuclear age—which encourages nations to develop separately rather than encouraging them to develop together?

The argument about taxes, too, concerns freedom and incentives. Taxes are necessary evils. And American multinationals, in overwhelming proportions, are not against paying taxes. Indeed, they are exemplary taxpayers in many countries where tax-dodging is standard corporate behavior. The argument isn't even about whether taxes should go up or down. All taxes, including corporate taxes, are costs of doing business and must be ultimately passed along as higher prices to consumers. That is a law of economics.

What the argument is about is whether the U.S. tax code will tax U.S. corporations at rates that are markedly different from the rates at which foreign governments tax foreign multinationals. America is by no means the only nation with MNCs: consider Shell, Phillips, Nestlè's, Michelin, Sony. There is nothing inherently wrong with, say, the elimination of the tax credit for foreign taxes, if such were the standard applied to every nation. But that is not the world standard. If the U.S. government applied it to American corporations, while the German government did not apply it to German corporations, it would ultimately reduce incentives for U.S. corporations to invest overseas. (The German corporations, retaining their foreign tax credit, could operate more efficiently in foreign markets, price their goods lower, and capture ever-larger market shares.) *German* corporations would earn the fifteen percent in Italy making widgets, while American corporations were earning much less at home. Soon, American corporations might even decide to invest their profits in the shares of German corporations. After all, a piece of a corporation earning fifteen percent on invested capital is better than a piece of a corporation earning only six percent. From labor's point of view, of course, this would be a real catastrophe. The dollars would still be invested overseas, as in Acme Widget's original plan, except that now:

- Most of the profits wouldn't return to the U.S.

- No American-made sub-assemblies for the widgets would be exported.

- No American-made machinery for a new factory would be exported.

- Certain economies of scale would be lost to American corporations, ultimately driving up consumer prices.

Of course, there is a way to prevent this, as our activist colleague noted. The government still might impose controls over the investment of dollars abroad by U.S. corporations and by American citizens, not just investment in new factories, but "portfolio" investment in foreign securities as well. Other nations do that, especially the backward and badly run ones. Such walls would surely keep the dollars here.

The trouble is that such controls would strike another blow, and a serious one, at the rather shaky idea that America still has a free economy. If the government can tell a corporation not to build a factory overseas, and if the government can tell an individual or a corporation not to invest dollars in foreign securities, then what else can the government tell you about how to spend your money? (Of course, the government calls it "investment capital," to make it sound more formal and less personal.)

The answer is: The government can tell you everything. Wisdom doesn't begin at the water's edge. So the government soon will tell you what kind of domestic investments you can make. ("America doesn't need another beauty cream product; America needs mass transportation, so let's penalize capital that flows into unconstructive channels.") When the government steps in to run the economy, everyone loses, especially the consumer. The people lose the ability to participate in dollar democracy.

The evidence is visible all over the world. Whenever a government body takes over economic decision-making, the people suffer. The ultimate economic desolation can be seen in the Soviet Union. There we see a populous, resource-rich land, peopled by folk who have in many instances demonstrated to the world just what the word "creative" means—and because of their insane regime, they can't even feed themselves. Why can't they feed themselves? Because the government doesn't allow farmers either freedom or incentives. Under the czars, Russia was the breadbasket of Europe but now agricultural productivity is amazingly low. Roughly a third of the Soviet Union's entire labor force is engaged in farm work, compared with only four percent in the U.S. Why are there shortages in all the Russian shops? Why are there long queues in front of all the shops? Because the government doesn't allow merchants freedom or incentives.

The Western societies do generally allow the economic creativity and efficiencies that flow from individual freedom and incentives. But as the great economist Joseph Schumpeter pointed out, capitalism's success may have within it the seeds of its own destruction. Affluent capitalistic societies spawn a well-to-do class of hypercritical intellectuals who diligently work to bring down capitalism. It is basically a power struggle. On one side are intellectuals who think that if they controlled the government they would make decisions so wise, so altruistic, so benevolent, that all society would revere and applaud them. On the other side is the free market, the quintessence of non-elitist democracy, a system that says the people know their self-interest better than the intellectuals.

All the plans described by my colleagues serve to undermine the market system and consequently undermine the ability of people to make their own decisions about their self-interest. Eroding the free market system leads inevitably not only to despotism, but, through inefficiencies, to poverty as well. That may sound overly dramatic and gloomy, but the evidence of modern history is on my side.

If our Activist friend has bad economics, his politics are incredible. He wants to redress what he claims is a political military imbalance by drafting the American multinationals into the Cold War and making them political tools of the American government. That would do two things, each worse than the other.

First, it would put still another large government obstacle in the path of the international businessman, making it much harder for him to perform his true economic function. In this instance, it would subject every business judgment and decision to the arbitrary second-guessing of a great superintelligence at the State Department who would say, no, sorry, you can't make that investment in New Zealand because New Zealand just sent its rugby team to South Africa and that upset the black governments in Africa, and we are courting the black governments in Africa, so you may not deal with New Zealand, nor for that matter, import their wool, or their mutton or whatever until further notice, or until the black African governments calm down.

But that's only the half of it. The policy you are advocating to bolster American foreign policy would, in fact, destroy it. As it is now, our multinational corporations are suspected of being imperialist agents of an imperialist American government, and are routinely denounced by the world's leftists. Just as routinely, and honestly, our MNCs deny these charges as leftist fantasies.

But under the banner of a neo-anti-Communism, our diplomatic friend proposed to make the fantasies literally true. Acme Widget will become a tool of the American government if we pursue this crazy scheme. Nothing could more surely play into the hands of the Soviet Union than to validate their malicious propaganda.

And there is something else. Both modern and ancient history teach that the use of economic harassment in peacetime rarely succeeds. Boycotts in a free world are just about unenforceable. If we don't sell to Rhodesia, someone else will. If the Arabs won't sell oil to us, we buy it from someone the Arabs will sell it to. If we won't give credits to the Soviet Union because we don't like their emigration policies, other governments are eager to give them credits and get the business and we then have zero leverage to influence their emigration policies. The Jackson Amendment, remember, reduced the number of Jews allowed to emigrate.

Not only doesn't "the wealth weapon" work, but people who suggest its use are also economic illiterates when it comes to understanding the situation in which such a weapon might be applied. We read in the press that the amount of trade between the U.S. and the Communist world has risen sharply. That is true in only the most limited sense. What has in fact happened is that our trade with the Communist nations has gone from nothing to next-to-nothing. As a trading partner with the U.S., the U.S.S.R. generally ranks down with Peru. Although we hear a great deal of talk about truck factories, computer technology and turnkey plants, the biggest single factor in our increased trade with the Communist world has been grain. Here are the numbers: In 1978 we exported only $4 billion to the Soviet Union and the Eastern bloc. But $1.4 billion of that represents grain. The trade with China is far less than that. By comparison, consider that our exports to Western Europe run $39 billion a year—almost ten times the amount of our dealings with Russia.

To my Activist friend, I say further that I am touched by your concern for human rights, and I am appreciative of your linkage of capitalism and freedom. I only wonder why you fail to note that economic freedom is a human right too—and yet you are preparing to sacrifice it on the altar of a revived Cold War.

The Activist's economic illiteracy is revealed in full flower in his "break OPEC" proposal. Preposterous. It can't work. America doesn't control enough oil buying power to make it work, not against the few countries that really count. Moreover, the technical problems are insurmountable: U.S. refineries require different grades of oil; in fact many were built to handle oil coming from specific foreign crudes, another reason the Godfather approach wouldn't work. I am in fact shocked by my Activist friend's failure to mention another aspect of the international oil companies. To some large measure they are responsible for the burgeoning prosperity of the world these last few decades. It was their technology, their capital, their marketing skills that put an energy source on every street corner in the world. They are directly and indirectly responsible for a great deal of what we call progress: electrification, mobility, transportation, revolutionized agriculture and so on. I say, hats off to them, and to the other multinationals that have similarly helped to give birth to the modern world, a radically better world.

And speaking of economic illiteracy, let me mention, just once, a hallowed sentence that embodies economic sanity: There is no free lunch. You can't have exports without imports, Mr. Labor Leader. You can't help American working people by raising the cost of goods they buy, Mr. Labor Leader. You can't promote internationalism and the fruits of an international marketplace by destroying it, Mr. Activist. No free lunch—you can't have it both ways.

There is one thing more to be considered before boasting of this so-called "wealth weapon." It is this: Don't we enhance its effectiveness by increasing our trade with the Communists?

It has become fashionable in the past couple of years to knock détente and Nixon and Kissinger. But, in fact, there was, and is, much to recommend the central notions of détente. One of those notions is that the U.S. can have no economic leverage unless there is some economic activity between East and West upon which to exercise such leverage. That means we have to create more trade and more investments in the Communist world; it means we must create what Henry Kissinger referred to as a "web of interdependence." That web will provide an organic and usable form of power, with no bellicose economic pressure tactics needed or desired. A Communist world dependent on the West for food, technology, and markets for their own products will not choose to be aggressive or mean-spirited. It would not be in their own best interests. What would be in their best interest would be to keep it cool. That would promote world peace, and let us remember that promoting world peace is still the number one goal of American foreign policy.

Like it or not, détente was, and still is, the official policy of our government. One aspect of that policy was to encourage increased commercial contacts between the two superpowers. American businessmen were asked to please go do it for the benefit of their country and world peace. They were told that by an elected president of this nation. They did just that—and promptly were described as greedy, craven, immoral scoundrels.

Very unfair.

Finally, some words must be addressed to our anguished friend from the developing world. I will say it bluntly, not because I do not sympathize with his difficult plight, but just because I do. To hold out false hope of easy solutions would be the ultimate unkindness. And the panaceas that have been mentioned—new OPECs, taxes on the rich, an international New Deal, commodity arrangements, not based on market forces—are all forms of economic methadone. The developing world has to go cold turkey. Kick the habit. And recognize the blunt central truth of the global economic system, which may sound familiar: there is no free lunch.

All the prattling about new imperialism and Western exploitation is wholly away from the main point. All the charity in the world, all the conscience money in the world (even if merited, which is doubtful) will not solve the economic problems he described. These will not solve hunger, or rural-to-urban-migration, or explosive population growth, or the dilemmas imposed by inefficient and inherently weak one-crop economies. Neither will the much-heralded "New International Economic Order."

Now, let me make myself clear. There is nothing wrong with wanting big change. In fact, I must say I favor a reordering of wealth in the world. It is neither desirable nor moral for more than half of the world's people to live in conditions of squalor.

But this cruel dilemma will be resolved only from within. Most of the poor nations in the world are not poor because of lack of resources or capital or because of the denial of fair terms of trade. Poverty in the developing world is not caused by the rapaciousness of multinational corporations. (And in fact, according to World Bank data, the developing world has made sharp gains in recent decades.) Multinationals help cure poverty; they do not create it.

The root cause of poverty lies in culture. When a national culture idealizes life in the hereafter at the expense of hard work in this world, when a national culture idealizes opium or sacred cattle, or voodoo—then it is a safe bet that little economic progress will be made. The underdeveloped society will not "take off" until its people want to, and are prepared to act as if they want to.

One example: less developed countries will continue to find it difficult to enter the fraternity of economically advanced nations until they are willing to treat commercial contracts as more than political scraps of paper than can be abrogated at the whim of a tin-hat dictator. It is positively malicious for governments in these countries to tell their populations that their poverty is due to exploitative foreign white devils. Poverty comes from within. It must be cured from within.

Now, mind you, I am not against various forms of aid going from rich nations to poor nations. In fact, I'm for it. It can be ameliorative. But it will not touch the root of the problem.

*   *   *

Labor Leader: The "wealth weapon" indeed! You have come up with a new name for "weakness." You call it "strength."

Multinational direct investment abroad has not created potential leverage for U.S. foreign policy. It has, rather, created an enormous domestic vulnerability.

Look at it this way. There is now about $130 billion in U.S. investments overseas. Even in slow years such as 1974 and 1975, this total grows by tens of billions of dollars. In addition, every year roughly $10 billion comes back to the U.S. in a "profit stream."

Now, all that American wealth, invested capital plus profit flow, is subject to the whim of foreign governments. In extreme instances they can nationalize American-owned companies. They can damn near tax them to death when they choose. They can harass and regulate them. They can prevent profits from being remitted back to the U.S. They can apply all these various pressures to make the companies and/or the U.S. government behave the way they, the foreigners, want us to behave. Did we have leverage on Iran—or did Iran have leverage on us because of all the billions we invested there?

After all, as the businessman has noted, in recent years, those profits earned overseas have comprised almost a third of the profits earned by the big American corporations. Those profits, says the businessman, help finance domestic investment. And all that is in the palms of the hands of foreign governments!

And what, in the area of direct investment, is our counterweight to all that? Foreigners' direct investments in the U.S. are only about one-fifth as large as ours overseas. Despite the buildup of OPEC dollars and the flight of politically frightened capital from Europe, the flow of direct investment is still basically one-way from the U.S. to the rest of the world.

That means our vaunted "leverage" amounts to the threat that we will withhold additional investments! Which would probably guarantee even harsher treatment of our existing investments and profit sources.

Some weapon! It is obvious that this bargaining equation plays out quite simply. They have the sticks. We have the carrots. I will tell you a little secret that I and some of my comrades in the labor movement have picked up during many years of collective bargaining. If you have a choice between carrots and sticks—take sticks.

So, direct investment overseas actually weakens our ability to use economic leverage overseas. We are doing nothing but multiplying the hostages we have given to foreign governments. The sooner we reduce such investment, the more leverage we will have.

For the United States does have a powerful form of economic power. It doesn't concern our willingness to invest in foreign lands. It does concern our willingness to let foreigners sell here in the United States. In that, at least, my Activist friend is correct.

Consider this potent source of leverage: No non-Communist developing nation has achieved real economic progress without having access to American markets. No developed nation in the free world has maintained its economic progress without access to

American markets. And now, Communist nations are beginning to realize the same thing: They can't reach a higher plateau of economic development unless they can sell to America to gain the dollars required to purchase the advanced technology they need.

Why is this market such a lure? Because we are 225 million people, all of whom are in a cash economy, most of whom have discretionary income available—and all participants in a continental common market that can be serviced in one language, through a coast-to-coast media system. By our own standards, we don't engage in a great deal of international trade, but what we buy represents an important part of total world trade.

Where, for example, would the Japanese motorcycle industry be without the American market? (We buy about a million motorcycles per year—and ninety-five percent of them are manufactured in Japan!)

What would happen to Peru and Bolivia if the United States stopped importing tin?

What would happen to the Italian shoe industry, or the New Zealand wool growers, or Ivory Coast coffee growers or Brazilian automobile radio manufacturers if the U.S. suddenly pulled the plug?

Now *that's* the real source of our economic power. Here, in this market, we can rap knuckles with an economic stick rather than ineffectively wave economic carrots. Other nations perfectly understand this approach because that's the way they manage access to their own domestic markets.

Moreover, this principle was precisely the one underlying the much-misunderstood Jackson Amendment. By linking "Most Favored Nation" tariff status to Soviet emigration policy, the equation was clearly established: access to American markets would be denied unless a specific U.S. foreign policy objective was achieved. That policy should be a model for other policy initiatives.

Let me add something else. If you suspect me of an ulterior motive in strongly endorsing this one aspect of the wealth weapon, you would be half-right. Although it is unquestionably the strongest arrow in our economic quiver, it also might have the effect of reducing the inflow of cheap imports into the United States, especially from low-wage developing countries and from the semi-slave economies of the Communist bloc. That would be desirable for all the reasons suggested earlier, beginning with the the defense of American jobs and living standards.

So, labor's position on the use of economic power is mixed. We favor it; but favoring it does not mean expanding our multi-national business presence around the world, as the Activist suggests might happen. Far from it.

Of course, it is obvious that big businessmen will oppose any form of increased government regulation over MNCs. One of their standard arguments has been heard here, a dreary and familiar theme in business rhetoric.

Businessmen always say: "But if we are restricted from doing thus-and-so, then the other multinationals, from other countries, will step in, and get the business." This line is invariably used to discourage any official flexing of our national economic muscle. "If we cut off Russia, then France and Germany will get the Russian business," the businessmen whine. The same line is used to defend tax loopholes: "If we don't have tax credits then the French and the German corporations, which do have tax credits, will get the business because they'll be able to produce goods cheaper."

And so it goes, The Economic Law of the Other Guy. There is, of course, some validity to it. But there is also a great deal of speciousness to it.

When business propagandists discourse about "the other guy getting the business," they always cite examples: the English, the French, the Germans, and the Japanese. It sounds like there are dozens and scores of "other guys" around ready to sell computers to the Soviets or build an up-to-the-minute plant in the Workers' Paradise.

The facts are quite different. The big league of international investing and trading is much smaller, and far more exclusive, than "free trade" propaganda makes it sound. Ninety-five percent of foreign direct investment is made by only eight countries! Those countries are the United States (with fifty percent of the total each year), Japan, the United Kingdom, Germany, France, the Netherlands, Sweden, and Switzerland. That's it: Just eight including the U.S. And every one of those other seven is tightly linked to the United States in what may be considered the Western economic bloc. The United States, if it chooses to use it, has economic, military, and diplomatic leverage that can be used to push these nations into concerted action. For example: If the United States were to determine that selling the Russians a whole truck factory complex (as at the Kama River facility) was potentially harmful to the military security of the West—is there really any doubt that we could prevent our allies from dealing with the Russians?

The Communists have bought heavily on credit, piling up a total

Soviet bloc debt to the West of some $50 billion. According to a simple rule of thumb, used by international bankers, the amount of debt-service—that is, interest and principal payments—due annually should not exceed fifteen percent of the borrowing country's hard-currency earnings from exports. By this standard, the Soviet bloc is a bad risk. In fact, some of its members are probably bankrupt, although they are still able to borrow in the export-hungry West.

Western bankers and businessmen and their governments should cease doing the Russians such extraordinary, unreciprocated favors. And the U.S. should insist that we stop helping our potential adversaries become too strong too easily.

George Ball, who was a top contender for the secretary of state's portfolio in the Carter cabinet, has put the policy imperative bluntly: "We should not continue to bail out Soviet food deficits, or help improve their industrial competence, or supply capital to develop their natural resources unless they stop exploiting situations of local conflict—or, in their jargon, assisting wars of national liberation. In addition, if we are to continue to act out the charade of détente, we must insist that they cooperate with us and the other industrialized nations to solve common world problems."

Ball, incidentally, has become a highly successful investment banker since his last tour of duty in Washington. Businessmen who pay for his hardnosed advice in the economic sphere ought to respect it in statecraft even more.

So the U.S., if it dismissed the business line about "the other guy," could demand that the West politically coordinate its trade and investment policies toward the East. And within the very small inner circle of the OECD, we unquestionably have the means to make our demand stick—if we have the will.

Another example of business dissembling might be called the Acme Widget Argument. Every time good old Acme Widget is not allowed to do anything and everything it wants to, when it wants to do it, the business community cries out in unison that such interference will surely lead to a regimented society that will never be able to discover antibiotics or computers.

That is bunk. Consider the specific Acme Widget example mentioned earlier. First we are led to believe that if Acme Widget can't invest in Italy, it won't invest in a bigger or better widget plant in the U.S. (because the market is "saturated"), nor will it or should it go into new fields in the U.S. (because it doesn't "know the business").

Well, maybe. (And maybe not.) But then we are told that poor old Acme will have to put its extra money in sterile places—like increasing its dividends. The company (read: management) won't even have access to the money if it pays it out in dividends. And what's bad for Acme is bad for America, or so we are told. Dividends, we're told, are inferior to entrepreneurial investments. They don't lead to miracle drugs or computers.

Bunk. They do. Economics is the science that deals with life at the margin, with replacements, with alternate strategies. It is a symptom of business short-sightedness that Acme's analysis goes no further than the idea that dividends are "sterile." That money, and the real investment capacity it represents, stays in the American economy. It may slosh around a bit, from a bank to a home mortgage, which enables a builder to build more homes, which provides a market to someone else who happens to be designing a solar home heating plant to be used as original equipment on new homes. Similarly, the dividend check may well be spent by an Acme stockholder who wants to buy shares in a brand new firm that will one day produce—Eureka!—miracle drugs.

The important point is that a hundred cents of each dollar stays in the United States. Compare that to a hundred cents going to Italy and then dribbling back here at the rate of fifteen cents a year while the original dollar finances an Italian solar heating plant and a new Italian miracle drug company.

If one understands the ubiquity and fecundity of the investment dollar when left in America, this same principle also demolishes other business arguments. For example, businessmen claim that foreign profits are now needed to feed American corporations the dollars required for domestic investment. Again, that may be true in some cases, but it simply doesn't add up if you view the process from a comprehensive national point of view.

Business has consistently underinvested in the United States because faster bucks beckoned overseas. While finance capital flowed to the biggest profit opportunities, our physical capital—domestic plant and equipment—became more obsolete and less competitive. And this, in turn, guaranteed that the best profit opportunities would always be "somewhere else." And that further starved investment here. For example, the age of our industrial capacity is roughly twice that of our major competitors such as Japan. Data indicate that almost seventy percent of Japan's machine tools are less than ten years old. Only thirty-five percent of ours are less than ten years old. No wonder they are outproducing us!

Other business arguments presented here are equally shoddy. For example, I guess we will hear endlessly about how wonderful it is that Volkswagen decided to build a plant in New Stanton, Pennsylvania. But the facts are that neither the German government, nor German unions, and consequently German corporations, are quite as magnanimous as their American counterparts. When it became apparent that Volkswagen could halt its loss of the U.S. market and compete effectively only by opening up an American plant, the German unions and the German government laid down very specific ground rules. Accordingly, the New Stanton plant cannot properly be called a manufacturing facility. It is more correctly an assembly facility. Engines, chassis, wheels, et cetera, will still be produced in Germany and exported to the U.S. Japanese auto manufacturers are expected to follow a similar strategy.

Compare that to the American style of idiocy. Our corporations build a plant overseas, set up a manufacturing operation and often send completed parts back to the U.S. as imports, which throw still more Americans workers on the scrap heap!

And what can we say to our friends from the Third World? We can say "good luck." We can say that their luck will indeed be good if they understand that the key to economic progress rests not with keeping wages low at home (in order to manufacture cheap goods for foreign subsidiaries) but by setting in motion a chain of events that raises wages at home. Only when the working class has some money does a real domestic market develop. And national wealth only begins its snowball effect when workers have the means to buy the goods they produce. That is the real analogy to the New Deal that the Third Worlders ought to understand. The reforms of the 1930s laid the groundwork for the social progress of the 1950s and 1960s. Progress came as wages climbed, not when workers were offered on a tray to the lowest bidder.

One way to raise wages is by developing a strong, free trade union movement. That surely has been the experience in the United States. Repression of the labor movement was a standard position of big business at least through the 1930s. Such repression was, at the least, accepted by the government up until the presidency of Franklin Roosevelt.

But despite business opposition and government indifference, a free trade union movement did develop in the United States. It developed because the courageous men who created the union movement, backed by millions of workers, finally won the power of collective bargaining and were able to raise wages to decent levels. And all that did was to create in America the single most important economic fact of our era: the biggest, richest consumer market in the world. Tens of millions of them are union members, who, incidentally, provide a free ride for most of the rest of the labor force in the matter of wage standards.

So we will confine our advice to our working class brethren in the developing world to a single word: organize. Don't let your so-called leaders sell your sweat cheap to foreigners.

Now, let me say a word about guilt. My colleague from the developing world harks back to an era when Cecil Rhodes bestrode the world like a colossus, when the sun never set on the British empire, when England and France would arbitrarily carve up distant continents, when little Holland and Belgium could dominate huge empires half a globe away—all the while ravaging native cultures and civilizations. For this, we are told, we are guilty and we must pay. We must pay by renegotiating or waiving debts owed us, we must pay by granting unrestricted and nonreciprocal free access to Western markets, we must pay for the creation of commodity reserves so that junior OPECs might be formed to work against us. Most important, we must pay by striking our breasts, confessing guilt for our past and present imperial plundering, and making open-ended moral as well as financial reparations.

Well, forget it. First of all, the anti-imperialists who peddle guilt to soft-headed Western intellectuals don't have history on their side. It is not an accident that those nations most touched by a colonial presence are the very nations that have developed most rapidly while those least touched have remained the most backward.

But there is more. At the time when all this imperial rapaciousness was going on, the ancestors of the men and women of the American labor movement were typically not involved in the slave trade, they did not own factories in England, and they were not colonialists building rubber plantations in Malaya. Far more typically, their ancestors were serfs in Poland or the Ukraine, or persecuted Jews, or Irishmen being poisoned by eating diseased potatoes, or Sicilian peasants trying to eke a livelihood from some of the harshest land in the world.

So neither we, nor our ancestors, would be the guilty ones even if there were guilt to be assumed. Moreover, we reject the entire concept of intergenerational guilt or of guilt by nationality. If the greatgrandfather of a Carolina textile worker owned slaves, it is not accurate to assess blame unto the fourth generation nor is it equitable to ask for reparations. So too, if the grandfather of an American worker owned a Cuban sugar plantation, it is not equitable to assess reparations to the contemporary worker for the alleged sins of his grandfather. Nor is it fair to assess reparations on American citizens today, all American citizens, not just union members, on the grounds that the U.S. government a hundred years ago may have committed economic abuses on the underdeveloped world (although on a microscopic scale compared to the European powers).

I use the word "reparations" because no matter how it is disguised, that in fact is what the developing nations demand. They plead past injustice and demand present repayment. And the repayers, of course, are not the giant corporations who commit the alleged exploitation. The repayers are the American taxpayers, working men and women who have to make up the money used to purchase commodities at inflated prices, and who have to make up indirectly the money the banks will not collect on waived debts. And the repayers are working men in the manufacturing sector who will lose their jobs to low-wage workers producing goods for the American market at preferential tariff rates that are nonreciprocal.

So, we reject the assumption of guilt. We are prepared to deal as equals with our counterparts in the developing world. No less, and no more. And their problem, we would submit, is not primarily with the developed world. Their complaint against MNC bribery and corruption, I must say, is more than a little ironic. I feel no inclination to come to the defense of the business community on this issue but this matter indirectly affects us as well.

It is well known, of course, that the nations crying loudest about corruption and bribery are just those nations where corruption and bribery in everyday life are endemic. But that kind of corruption is only the tip of the iceberg. It is the Third World governments that are so often the true corrupters and bribers. They corrupt by preaching democracy and repressing every aspect of it including the free trade union movement. And they are the true bribers in the relationship with multinational corporations. Their bribes to the MNCs are not in money alone; they take the form of complex enticements. Come and invest in sunny Pepoto, they say. Come here and pay no taxes for twenty years. Come here and build your plant on free land. Come here and pay no tariffs. Come here and repatriate 100 percent of your profits. Come here and don't worry about unions or minimum wage laws. And they then cry economic rape!

That's not rape, friends. That's economic whoredom masquerading as latter-day "comparative advantage." These governments grant favors to foreign firms that they do not grant to their own local enterprises—all in an effort to bribe capital away from the opportunities elsewhere to which it would flow if the unfettered laws of economics were allowed to work. Instead, we see those champions of classical free economics, the corporations, lured by artificial incentives to government-controlled economies, while the same corporations condemn any degree of government influence at home.

Nor does the demand for giveaways come only from the poor nations. Incredibly enough, we now hear it from our dear friends, the European Communists! For years, as noted earlier, they drank deeply at the trough of Western credit, lavishly extended by Western governments and banks. Now, suddenly, the Communists are wondering what belts to tighten in order to pay off their mountain of debts. They have come up with a wonderful idea. They will tighten our belts! Tightening our belts for their gain involves suggesting (demanding?) something called a "rescheduling of debt." In plain English that means welshing. Part of the "rescheduling" involves restructuring the old debt so that the new debt will only call for one percent or two percent interest. That, in a world of mostly double-digit interest rates, is almost free money! And then our bankers will lend the reduced interest due! As the game nears a climax in Communist Europe, it is just getting under way in Red China, where the Communists are renting their very cheap labor to the capitalists in return for credits and direct investments.

So here we are: Western multinational companies and banks, using Western government credits, send entire factories, technologies and modes of production to nations banded together for the sole, publicly announced purpose of one day crushing our system, and, finally, we are asked to further liberalize the terms of this arrangement so that they are relieved of the costs of doing us in!

That's crazy! And the irony of this craziness is that, once again, the person who ultimately pays the cost of such international high finance is the ordinary citizen, workingman, and taxpayer. Well, we're not going to let it happen. There is one other basic difference between Labor's gains in New Deal days compared to what the Third Worlders want to do now: we had the vote in America. Electoral muscle made it happen. The LDCs, I point out, don't vote in the U.S. And we didn't get to where we are by voting against our best interests.

*   *   *

Foreign Policy Activist: To the gentleman from the Third World I have this to say: Don't threaten. Theatrics have poisoned the relationship between the rich and the poor nations for well over a decade now. It is fruitless rhetoric because it is so unreal. The tribesmen of darkest Africa will not swim the Atlantic to invade Long Island. Indian peasants will launch no atomic attacks on San Diego.

And the economic threats are not much more credible. Except for oil, no Third World resource cartel is credible. Even the oil threat is only potentially harmful, not devastating. American firms are drilling oil in Texas, Alaska, California, the North Sea, Canada, and other places. We sit on an abundance of natural gas. We have an even greater abundance of coal. We have minerals and other industrial commodities in abundance. We can survive.

Therefore, threats do not form a credible basis for North-South or rich-poor negotiations. Nor does history. Most of the underdeveloped nations were primitive tribal societies long before Western colonialism touched them. It is not our duty to change the fabric of history. We don't owe anyone anything. We will not be bullied into charity and we will not be bullied into what has been called reparations.

There is only one basis upon which nations ought to conduct negotiations and that is mutual self-interest. As it happens, there is a mutual self-interest between the rich nations and the poor nations. It consists of helping poor nations help themselves to become nonpoor nations. That is to the long range benefit of the wealthy nations not because we are afraid of vituperative United Nations resolutions or commodity cartels, and not because we are prepared to assume the burden of retroactive intergenerational guilt.

There are sound reasons for the rich to help the poor. One is surely humanitarianism. And the second is economic. In the long run, from a half-dozen points of view, nothing could be better for Western economies than for the developing countries to move toward full-fledged consumer economies. It would create new markets and a tremendous demand for Western goods and services while at the same time wage differentials would be narrowed. A perfect combination.

This is surely a fairer basis for dealing with one another than the hypocritical selfishness of the super-rich OPEC extortionists, who give their poor brothers of the Third World emotional rhetoric, while blighting their hopes for development. OPEC is not a model for the Third World, but a profoundly destructive menace.

So, we expect to cooperate with the nations of the Third and Fourth Worlds, but we will not be bullied, nor will we push our multinational companies into situations where they will be bullied, nor will we give up our sovereign right to use our economic power as an instrument of national policy in the international arena.

This is scarcely a new idea. As our business colleague has pointed out, it is as old as history. What appears to be radically new, and shocking to some people, is the idea that America has the right to behave as other nations do, according to its own self-interest and without any apologies for throwing its weight around. What I have called "the wealth weapon" is so obvious as to be commonplace in Great Britain, France, Germany, or Japan, all of which routinely adjust their international economic policies to their political and strategic priorities. No one criticizes them or the Russians, but we Americans have been afraid to be caught even thinking about our national self-interest.

That day, friends, is over. The international events of the past decade have brought Americans back to their senses. Vietnam is over. Over. We have seen Soviet encroachment in Africa, in the Middle East, in the "crescent of crisis." We have seen our interests erode; we have seen one too many American embassies evacuated under duress, too many hostages bullied. I say: enough. My American countrymen say: enough. We will do what we must to protect our interests. We will use the tools that are available, military, political, and economic. The "wealth weapon" is available.

*   *   *

Third World Leader: I must say I am shocked. You all sit here screeching at each other and I am amused when I look at you. You wear handsome, well-tailored clothes—even and especially the representative of the toiling masses, my friend from the labor movement. You have all attended the finest universities, as do your children. You eat in splendid restaurants and dine by candlelight at elegant parties. You live in stately homes with aquamarine swimming pools.

And you preach to the people in the developing world as if they were small businessmen at a Chamber of Commerce luncheon in Plains, Georgia. A little gumption, fellows! A little get-up-and-go! When the going gets tough, the tough get going!

Our Activist is if anything, the worst of the lot. He brandishes his supposed "wealth weapon." Do you really need more leverage to force the destitute people of the developing world to do the bidding of the majestic United States? Shame on you!

What smug lecturers you are! You have grand theories of power and economics and forget that the objects of your theories are desperately poor people, so poor, so disadvantaged as to be far beyond your Western comprehension.

There are one million villages in India! Their residents live in cramped thatch dwellings, steaming hot in the summer, chilly in the winter, without running water or electricity or toilets. Without decent food. Without books. Without newspapers. Without television. Without medical services to deal with the most crippling parasitic diseases. And without hope. These are the people to whom you direct your go-getter lectures and at whom you aim your threats. For shame!

American-style individualistic capitalism, a style of life perhaps suited to a situation of man-versus-the-frontier, does not work in huts of black Africa where a tribal culture holds sway. You can't give forty-acres-and-a-mule to a favela dweller in a South American slum who has just left his mule behind in the countryside. Since the time of the American sod-busters, farming has become a capital-intensive industry that demands tractors and tube-wells and new seeds and fertilizers. And the South American peasant has no capital for a tractor.

Don't sell your labor cheap to foreigners, says the American labor baron. Good advice, but irrelevant. How is one to live? Not on theories but with a job. And we have no jobs—unemployment in some countries of the developing world is near fifty percent! And you complain about six percent or seven percent!

Jobs don't come without capital. We'll take that capital from MNCs—surely. Even if, as the American labor spokesman says, we have to use "bribery" to get it. "Bribery," of course, is his word; in the academic world the same phenomenon is described as "national economic policy."

But, friends, the truth is that we need more capital than we will ever get from the profit-seeking investments of the multinational corporations. Much more. We need hundreds of billions of dollars if our people are ultimately to live decent lives.

Answer your own question: "What kind of world do you want?" Do you want a world ruled by starvation and pestilence and illiteracy? Do you want a world where two-thirds of the population lives in desperation, ripe for violence and revolution? Do you want a world where the desperate two-thirds will have to take what they need from the one-third who have it? Not long ago, when the lights went off in New York City, the poor in the slums stole everything they could get their hands on—and the rich were shocked. I believe that the poor behaved rationally, as they will on a world-wide scale if they have the chance.

Now, you say that we are asking for charity and handouts. And we say that we have been victimized. And we continue to be victimized. The rich nations take and waste far more of the world's resources than can be justified by any standard of "fairness." Americans spend more to feed their pampered pet animals than some developing countries earn to support themselves. Any realistic sense of equity demands that we receive, and truly deserve, compensation for past ills. (You call it "reparations"—and maybe that's not such a bad word.) And we also truly deserve a more equitable share of present income and wealth.

But the real fact of the matter is that it doesn't matter. Whether it is charity or reparations, earned or unearned, does not change the fact that in the next quarter of a century hundreds of billions of dollars must change hands between the rich and the poor living on this small planet.

Otherwise, there will be catastrophe for all—rich and poor.

If you don't like our suggested instrumentalities for this necessary transfer of wealth—new terms of trade, tapping the IMF, sea-bed royalties and so on—propose other ones. But the bottom line must add up to hundreds of billions of dollars.

The clock is ticking.

8.

Who's Right, Who's Wrong?

We have heard four self-interested parties make their cases—passionately, even eloquently and intelligently. But what are the interests and conclusions of the authors?

Serene, wise, all-knowing, we seek only the national interest and the global interest. Does that sound familiar? Isn't that what all these other fellows say they are interested in? Aha! But we are objective. We have no profit sheet to worry about, no constituents out of work, no political movements to galvanize, no starving masses to deal with. Our interests are solely directed to that key question: "What kind of world do we want?"

And to that question, it is now appropriate to add another one: "How do we get there?" And another: "Who's right—the Businessman, the Labor Leader, the Activist, the Third Worlder?"

Surely, such serene, objective observers will be able to answer those questions and the others that have been raised in this volume. Surely.

The Authors Speak:

As we said in the beginning, this is a book about on-going arguments, not final answers, and the authors have argued at length with each other as well as by proxy with our composite characters trying to impose what the reader rightly expects: a set of tidy conclusions.

Sorry. There will be no definitive answer to the question: "Who's right—the Businessman, the Labor Leader, the Third Worlder or the Foreign Policy Activist?" It would be satisfying to claim that an ultimate truth, or even an ultimate opinion, emerged from this four-cornered argument. It would also be inaccurate.

They are all right—about some things. Everyone has a point.

The vastly complicated subject of "multinational corporations" does not lend itself to unassailable generalizations. The subject matter encompasses the realms of political science, trade policy, international economics, diplomacy, defense, and domestic politics. Particularly, domestic politics. Experts are most comfortable with small pieces of this vast territory—and even they argue with each other. Just try to get one definitive/expert consensus opinion about whether jobs related to exports truly make up for, or more than make up for, job losses due to imports! As for us, we leave the experts behind; we began this project as nonexperts and have preserved our status.

Still, as nonexpert generalists we have travelled and read and interviewed on this subject for three years. If we haven't solved, with data and balance sheets, the problems we have dealt with, we have at least come up with some opinions, and a sense of how the land lays. These views, this sense, we now share with the patient reader.

Well, then, what kind of world do we want? To begin, it should be a world where the standard of living is generally rising. But bread is inescapably bound up with economic freedom.

Our work has convinced us that large, modern, far-flung international corporations are a central force that lifts the global standard of living. Far better than their antagonists, they deliver on their promises to consumers, in large measure because they must strive daily to keep their favor in the marketplace. In at least that sense, then, we accept the basic business argument.

We believe that the MNC has, in the past third of a century, worked surprisingly well for all concerned. It has been instrumental in bringing capital, technology, expertise and large-scale organization to the less developed countries. Without such activity, it is hard to imagine many of the advances in health, agriculture, productivity, electrification and transportation that have in fact occurred in these countries since World War II.

The MNC has also worked well for the rich and highly advanced countries, particularly the United States. By stimulating manufacturing and importing from low-wage countries, MNCs have helped provide lower-cost goods for American consumers. In many industries, particularly high wage industries, they have also stimulated domestic employment—at least through the first three-and-a-half decades since World War II. And for themselves and their stockholders, of course, MNCs have made handsome profits and built global economic enterprises.

From a diplomatic point of view, the MNC has surely been a force for world peace. While we reject the glib claim that increased trade (say, with the Soviets) is automatically a step toward peace, it is clear that as a general proposition increased economic activity between nations leads toward a more stable and perhaps peaceful world. Nations dependent upon one another for capital, food stuffs, technology and markets are probably somewhat less likely to blow up one another and are probably somewhat more likely to understand each other's point of view.

So, the MNCs have, as they claim, helped raise the standard of living, and helped international harmony. Beyond all that, however, there is something else to be said in the MNC's favor, at least from the authors' point of view. The authors (as the observant reader should by now have discerned) are deeply concerned about the outcome of the ideological struggle unfolding in the world. The kind of world we want is not only peaceful, not only a world with a rising standard of living, but one with a rising standard of freedom.

In preserving freedom, America has played a unique role in the world in recent decades. In many ways, admittedly often acting in concert with other institutions, the MNC has helped Americanize the world.

We regard that as good, and important. The development and expansion of MNCs has sent American technology to every part of the world. With that technology has gone an American-style of production, distribution, marketing, advertising and communications—typically keyed to mass production and mass consumption. This general process has not only sent American investment dollars all over the world, but with them, Americans to keep a wary eye on how things are going.

And this process, of course, has affronted and offended many intellectuals abroad who find America troubling and fear the spread of American values based on consumer power and democracy in their own societies. Anti-Americanism, as Eric Hoffer has re-

marked, is a virulent global disease found among would-be aristo-
crats who are repelled by the triumph of the ordinary man in
America.

We endorse the contention of Seymour Martin Lipset that Amer-
icanism is an ideology, not just another form of nationalism. That
is a key reason, says Lipset, why our politics have never been as
sharply divergent or as class-ridden as have been European politics. A broad ideological consensus reigns here across almost the
entire political spectrum, and across the whole class spectrum.
That American consensus is hard to pin down, but it deals in large
part with the nature of man and society. Americans believe, almost
without thinking about it, that ordinary people have a right politically to determine their own destiny, and to rise to a higher station
by merit, not by breeding or class. Americans believe that technology, modern techniques of production and distribution, and diligent work, all operating in a free society, can lead these ordinary
folks to achieve an extraordinary standard of living.

As a nation, we have also come to believe that we will be able to
proceed along these paths of freedom and prosperity in future decades only if other national communities share some or all of these
principles. We have learned that we are not an island unto ourselves.

Finally, we have been grateful to learn that many people around
the world do indeed share these ideals that we had come to regard
as an American ideology. The real revolutionary insurgency in the
world has an American tap-root. In huts and villages in remote
corners of the world, the pictures on the wall are more likely to be
of Lincoln and Kennedy than of Lenin and Khrushchev.

This American ideology, in all its many manifestations, has
spread around the world through a variety of mechanisms: music,
art, literature, movies, clothing, scientific interchange, political interchange, shared histories—and, significantly, commerce typically
transmitted by the multinational corporation.

In their full variety these corporate giants have brought oil wells
(and prosperity) to a dozen poor nations, mass retail marketing
symbolized by Sears Roebuck in South America, rubber technology to build much of a national economy in Malaysia, sophisticated computer services and manufacturing best exemplified by
International Business Machines, airplanes, airports and airlines
that connect areas previously untouched by modernity to the rest
of the world, drugs to ward off an array of debilitating diseases,
reliable national telephone interconnections (sometimes through

the offices of archvillain International Telephone and Telegraph),
capital in a mighty torrent, the freshets fed by international banks
and, of course, a wide variety of manufacturing firms producing
goods ranging from shoes, to clothes, to baseballs, to tennis rack-
ets. And much, much more.

In each of these instances, and countless others, not only is the
service or product that is offered or produced inherently beneficial
in its own right, but it leads to the deposit of a piece of America in
another country. Wherever you travel in the entire world, the music of America follows you. It is young, vibrant, unconventional
and profoundly revolutionary because it liberates the senses of all
who hear and respond to its rhythms. Only a society becoming
freer can absorb its impact.

Because the ideas of the American ideology are so radical (encouragement of initiative, for example), this ideology spreads
across the globe. It has special appeal to the young and unestab-
lished, but not the radical. Our ideology does not demand heroism
from ordinary people at home or abroad. Because we know we
need allies, the spread of American ideology helps assure our own
survival as the kind of nation we want to be.

Now, this export of American values has its disquieting aspects—
which is why one species of intellectuals all over the world decry
"American cultural imperialism." It is not "multinationals" alone
that they abhor, but the certain and correct knowledge that the
MNCs never travel unencumbered. They transmit the seeds of a
different culture—materially more advanced, physically healthier,
psychologically hyperthyroid—and these seeds grow often in
strange, alien, sometimes hostile environments. Russian young people, too, want jeans and rock records and the free lifestyle they
connote. One day, the commissars worry, they might want other
things: to go into business for themselves(!) or even vote in a free
election.

It is important to note, however, that the germination of those
seeds of the American ideology is not an imposed phenomenon.
Almost without exception, it is sought after by the people of host
countries. Those same countries then view the phenomenon am-
bivalently, sometimes issuing harsh rhetorical broadsides, and then
continue to seek more investment because they know it is intrin-
sically beneficial.

From an American point of view, such ambivalence is probably
not necessary. If we view our country as the two-centuries-old
purveyor of a radical idea that needs a receptive world to survive,

the corporate instrumentality we call multinational business is on balance clearly beneficial.

So the business community is essentially correct when it says it is a scandal that something so beneficial is attacked as something so harmful.

Viewed from this cosmic perspective of What Kind of World We Want, many of the specific criticisms leveled at multinational corporations in recent years become irrelevant. Have some (many?) MNCs been involved in corporation-to-government bribery? Is that really evil, considering the "everyone does it" mentality of the people and governments of the host countries?

If so, then let the practice be outlawed, and the law enforced, and be done with it. It is not a major problem, although it makes headlines. It can be controlled if the host countries and the MNCs and the U.S. government want to control it, but it won't make much difference either way. Bribery has an ancient and dishonorable history, long antedating MNCs. It should not be the issue that determines whether MNCs are in fact useful instrumentalities to raise the standard of living or the standard of freedom.

So too with many of the other concerns raised about MNCs: They are not central to the big questions. Are tax policies unfair? Change them. Are accounting statements misleading? Standardize them and enforce them. Do MNCs ravage the local government in a search for resources? Forbid them. Do they pull too much capital from rich countries or too many profits from poor countries? Change the laws.

The governments involved, on both the investing and the host country side, have the *power* to do all that and more to the MNCs (as our Businessman has pointed out). Big corporations have a lot going for them, but not armies. Governments have power and can do to MNCs what they will, including totally destroy them.

But, in the process of making the rules and regulations under which MNCs exist, governments also are obliged to ask themselves questions: What kind of world do those governments want? How do they propose to go about raising the standard of living?

They can tax the MNC and regulate it, and harass it, and penalize it to their hearts' content, but those questions persist: How to raise the standard of living? What kind of world?

Simply put, we have come to believe there aren't any satisfactory answers to either question without a healthy and reasonably free concept of the multinational corporation working in a framework of generally free international trade. Overpenalizing and overregulating the MNC ultimately reaches a point where the company can no longer help create the conditions that are universally sought.

As we see it, for all its ills and flaws (and they surely exist), the twentieth century style, profit-oriented, multinational corporation has been a primary agent of a rising standard of well-being in the world. There is no known substitute for it, and no competitor that seems to have any chance of matching its successes. So we're for it.

We have said "on balance" multinationals are beneficial to the U.S. But like all human instrumentalities they are flawed, and we have a certain sympathy with the views of labor spokesmen.

Labor's case, recited here, asks not for an end to "free trade" nor for the dissolution of multinational enterprises, but only for moderation in terms of existing political/economic realities. There is no theoretical system so grand or perfect, the labor leaders seem to say, that can't be improved by tinkering and their position today is that of tinkerer, not a destroyer. They do not propose to be scared off by a word—"protectionist"—and neither do we.

When the labor folk say, "We'd be for real free trade if we could ever find any of it,"—they may exaggerate, but they also deal with a real world phenomenon. After all, businessmen and labor leaders alike have used the phrase "Uncle Sugar" to describe America's unreciprocated generosity in the world trading community. And the fact is that other governments do play a much broader role in controlling, directing and often subsidizing their foreign business activity. This, of course, undermines the concept of free trade, leaving American labor and business at a competitive disadvantage.

Accordingly, in a commercial world where free trade exists only as an abstract ideal and not as a practical reality, unions want America to behave in practical fashion which, as we have thought about it, strikes us as fair enough. The field of "political economy" must deal with politics as well as economics. And politics deals with "who gets what." Just as the other major industrial powers play a role in protecting their workers, their industries, and their markets, so too should the U.S., say the unionists.

As a matter of fact, this is what happens. Our national administrations talk about "free trade," while negotiating "OMAs" ("orderly marketing agreements") and "voluntary quotas" on a wide variety of imported goods ranging from shoes to cars to steel. Needless to say, a trading system of OMAs is not exactly what Adam Smith had in mind.

So, Big Labor, and not-so-big labor, too, wants a seat at the table where the shape of Imperfect Free Trade will be molded.

They see that the percentage of clothing sold in America that is produced in foreign countries has grown from five percent to thirty-five percent in the last fifteen years. They see that American garment workers are losing their jobs. They know better than anyone that what may be somewhat tolerable during a time of full employment (when a worker can switch jobs from clothing manufacture to, say, electronics piecework) is intolerable during a time of high unemployment when the only shift possible may be from the assembly line to the welfare line.

They see, too, that despite recession and high unemployment in the U.S., despite high levels of foreign investment in America, direct business investment abroad by American firms remains at near-record high levels. So unions make demands which, in all fairness, are rather moderate demands. They do not say, "Roll back the clock" to an earlier era when 95 percent of our clothing was produced in America. They say, instead, "Let's take steps to see to it that it doesn't get any worse!"

And they don't ask for help only in industries where the balance of trade is negative, that is, where imports exceed U.S. exports, as in clothing. The machinists, in contrast to the garment workers, basically *gain* rather than *lose* from liberal international trade. After all, the export of American airplanes (military and civilian) employs tens of thousands of machinists. So the machinists ought to be four-square for full free trade, right?

Wrong. The airplane workers gain jobs, but those machinists working in the electronics industry are threatened by imports. So they complain and lobby. When it is pointed out to those unions that gain from trade that, say, 90 percent of their members gain from free trade, they say, "If I have a healthy body and a sore foot, and I go to a doctor, I don't want him to tell me that 90 percent of my body is all right and just keep limping along. If he tells me that, I'll get a new doctor."

Substitute "congressman" for "doctor," count up the number of people with import-oriented sore feet, and one begins to understand why "protectionism" is a big, painful and continuing political issue. And so it must be viewed. It is not essentially an economic issue, but a political issue, inordinately complicated, involving competing interests, and each interest is laden with an overabundance of less-than-totally accurate rhetoric and data.

If, accordingly, we view the situation as a political process, rather than a philosophical contest that demands a clear and absolute outcome, we will all be more attuned to reality and also can sleep easier.

So: do not expect to reach a "solution." Expect to engage in a process, a worldwide process of continual adjustment to shifting political circumstances which aims at achieving tolerable temporary arrangements. That process should not be confused with anything resembling "pure free trade." Instead, it is "impure free trade," and in the bargaining process from which it emerges the labor unions from many nations are entitled to a place at the table.

This political process, of course, outrages some multinational businessmen who, like Greta Garbo, only want to be left alone. Gentlemen, that is not to be. Your businesses will be bullied, badgered, and bulldozed not only by labor unions and politicians, but by host country governments, journalists, intellectuals, and other assorted hangers-on. You may surely fight back, defending your real and legitimate interests in political-economic rough-and-tumble, understanding that you control only one seat at the bargaining table, not all of them. The pure and perfect world of free trade is not to be, and despite the sympathetic intent of works such as this one, multinationals will continue to be pilloried and abused.

Cry all the way to the bank, businessmen, but do not let your tears destroy you. Multinational businessmen will never be loved, no more than domestic businessmen are loved. But the basic process of international investment and trade will continue—only because no one can really do without it. Because the authors are both pundits and seers, we can predict the fate of multinational businessmen as a class. They will become both wealthier and more agitated.

If the authors accept large parts of the business and labor arguments, the same cannot be said for the case made by the Less Developed Countries. We take this position not because we feel no sympathy with the plight of the poor countries. There are hungry and unhealthy people in those nations, and we take our position precisely because we do feel sympathy with the have-nots of the world.

Now, there is a certain class of social and political fictions that men and societies live by that are erroneous, but not particularly harmful. A fantasizing left-liberal may say, for example, that Watergate represented a movement where proto-totalitarians, led by Richard Nixon, were planning to do away with civil liberties in America. The authors don't believe that's what Watergate represented. What it was was bad enough. But, as it turned out, the misguided left-wing view seems to do no real harm; the people who hold it, we assume, merely remain hyper-vigilant in their efforts to defend civil liberties.

But the untruths now abroad in the world about poor countries and rich countries are not harmless fictions. They are extremely pernicious and subversive fictions, and the people they harm, almost exclusively, are poor people. The great irony, of course, is that the fictions are perpetrated by the people who claim to be most deeply concerned about the welfare of the poor people.

To explain our position let us for a moment put aside the notions of guilt, morality, and equity. For one can argue endlessly about whether colonialism represented a heinous imperial ripoff or whether, to the contrary, it was responsible for introducing health care, technology, law and order, literacy and other aspects of civilization to the poor and backward countries. Similarly, the argument can continue endlessly as to whether current commodity prices are "equitable." The real question behind that question is this one: Is it fair that one man should receive $2 a day for his hard work while another man a half a world away gets $100 a day for his hard work? Even acknowledging that while both workers work hard, they do not by any means produce equal amounts of usable wealth? We eschew those arguments because they are essentially sterile: economic progress does not typically come about because of judgments about guilt, morality, and equity.

These are phony issues. The history of mankind does not reveal many (any?) instances where retroactive guilt feelings prompted contrition in the form of self-inflicted wounds. Thus, even if the poor countries could establish beyond a shadow of a doubt that the imperialists are responsible for their present dilemma, it would mean little. If all in the court of world public opinion agreed that commodity prices are far below "equity" scale, it would mean less.

Why? Because acceptance of those beliefs would require a massive transfer of wealth from one group of countries to another. That is a very unlikely occurrence when the putative donor countries are free and democratic, and when their leaders must face the voters at regular intervals.

Isn't it ironic that people possessed of a liberal mentality that has abstract sympathy for poor-country spokesmen in flowing robes preaching the coming of the New Economic Order—are also ready to take to the barricades as consumers to protest soaring coffee prices?

Bluntly stated: One cannot be for the Third World's definition of economic justice unless one is also for charging American poor people the equivalent of $10 for a pound of coffee. And American politicians who endorse $10 a pound coffee for their constituents can be described quite simply as "former politicians." They are losers.

Try as one might, it is impossible to suggest plausible public rhetoric that addresses an American factory worker earning $15,000 a year in this manner: "Pal, I know you're trying to keep up with house and car payments, and I know you're sending a child to college, but pal, you're a wasteful, materialistic glutton, suffering from an overabundance of goods. So we are going to make things even tougher on you and help the fellow growing yams in Togo." No matter how much flowery language is used to decorate the idea, it is clear that the New Economic Order involves a massive transfer of wealth which would make the "haves" poorer and the "have-nots" richer.

More important, it would do so through an abrogation of the economic system, the market system, that is perceived by the West as having made the "haves" somewhat well-to-do and the "have-nots" better off than they used to be.

There is only one way such an economic transfer could take place—through the application of raw power. History shows such transfers can work: Nation "A" conquers nation "B" and takes its wealth or enslaves its work force, as the U.S.S.R., at the end of World War II, conquered Eastern Europe, and then carted off whole factories as war reparations. Accordingly, the poor-country spokespersons routinely bluster about their power, about the inferno that will arrive if their demands are not met. We'll cause so much trouble, they say, that you might as well pay now.

Wrong. They can bluster all day long at the United Nations. But the troops of the joint Tanzanian-Indonesian-Ecuadorian armed expedition cannot plausibly be expected to land amphibiously at Miami Beach, preparatory to a northwest flanking movement to capture Washington, D.C. We purposefully make the threat concrete and therefore absurd.

Guilt-peddling won't work, and pleas for equity won't work, and raw power won't work. Accordingly, it is not "humanitarian" to

suggest the fiction that they will work. It is the opposite of humanitarian, it is downright harmful, to suggest strategies and tactics
doomed to failure when the people who ultimately suffer from the
overblown rhetoric and misguided strategies are the same poor
people who need to be helped.

Just as Western governments will not be shamed or bullied into
unilaterally surrendering their wealth, neither will the MNCs. Our
prescription for the poor countries is an elemental one: Live in the
real world, not in a fairy-tale world. For example, MNCs probably
can be squeezed for more as long as some basic rules are not violated: that they are not forced into unprofitability, that they are not
forced into a position where doing business elsewhere is more
attractive.

That does not offer total latitude, but it does offer considerable
latitude. Bargains can be driven about taxes and capital and royalties on technology. Such hard bargains are part of our everyday
international commerce. Such bargaining can also influence commodity pricing, occasionally dramatically, as in the case of OPEC.
But OPEC's strategy, unlike the fictional plans of the New International Economic Order, was based on real economic power (the
early unavailability of substitute fuels), not on the illusion of economic power. It certainly was not based upon massive charity,
which is the unstated first premise of the New Economic Order—a
fictional premise.

So that is one harmful fiction—and policy should not be based
on fiction, no matter how appealing. There is another harmful fiction afloat in the developing world. Our composite spokesman
brings it up: Don't blather about liberty, he says, we need food
first. We say to our Third World friend: That is not a trade-off. It is
social fiction and economic mythology to suggest (as is done so
often) that in the developing world authoritarian government
yields economic development faster than a freer society. Travel to
China and travel to Taiwan if you want to see the difference—one
(mostly free) Chinese nation already in the modern world, one Chinese nation (rigidly unfree) still in the age of the water buffalo.
(See also: North Korea vs. South Korea and West Germany vs. East
Germany.) It should be apparent by now that we believe that the
MNC can best be used as a development tool in a free economy.

Finally, what of our Activist's view of the role of the MCNs? The
authors are generally drawn to this general view, if not to each
specific program.

When this small work was begun in 1975 we suspected that an

economically-oriented international political strategy would have to evolve to meet new circumstances such as the U.S. retreat from Asia, the emergence of OPEC's petro-power as a leading force in world affairs, and the strains of inflation and resurgent nationalism within the generation-old Western alliance and trading system.

Consider again our straightforward thesis: The bedrock goal of American foreign policy is to preserve for the next generation that political environment in which "the Western notion of freedom" can best survive.

Until recently we had at least three things going for us toward this goal: We were the world's most powerful nation militarily, and in a few instances had demonstrated order-keeping credibility by using limited military force. We were the world's most influential diplomatic force. Nations all around the world adjusted their policies and politics to work in concert with the United States. Finally, we were the world's most potent economic force, and with our allies, dominated the global economy.

Things have changed. Independent analysts judge that the Soviet Union enjoys at least military parity with the United States, is becoming stronger in certain fields, and, perhaps may soon achieve a position of general military superiority. In Angola, on the horn of Africa, in Afghanistan, in Indochina, as well as Cuba, we see ominous signs of what newly expansionist Soviet military power means. Meanwhile, the Vietnam experience sent many policy-makers on a prolonged and debilitating guilt trip, effectively limiting any American response anywhere, almost regardless of the provocation. That same guilt complex set in motion a breast-beating process that gutted the ability of the CIA to help friends and discomfit our friends' adversaries.

So much for our military and quasimilitary posture. Things may improve, but we've got a long rebuilding process ahead of us. Diplomatically, the United States now confronts hostile majorities in every international forum—an unholy alliance of Communists and poor countries and OPEC nations. This often makes it more difficult to pursue the American goal of preserving a free international environment. Example: The U.S. is forced to counter serious diplomatic efforts to legitimize the muzzling of a free press—an effort that had United Nations sanction! And, of course, our military decline lessens our diplomatic influence.

Only the economic primacy of the West remains unimpaired, in fact enhanced. For the Marxist dream is dead, surely in its totalitarian aspects, strangled in the bureaucracies of Moscow, the ideological rigidities of Peking, and the bungled economics of scores of Third World countries on three continents. Meanwhile, the West not only retains its economic and technological lead (notwithstanding the recent recessions and inflations) but also the only non-OPEC developing countries to make major economic gains have all been operating on the Western model: Korea, Brazil, Taiwan, Malaysia, Mexico, to name a few. Furthermore, no developing nation has achieved a modern mass consumer society without access to Western technology and Western markets. That fact is now acknowledged by the Soviet and East European governments, which desperately seek access to both our technology and markets.

Hence, we have a goal, and we have tools to use. Some of our tools are bent and rusty, but others are gleaming and effective. The gleaming ones can be found under the general rubric of "economic tools."

Until quite recently only one vital element was missing from the new strategy: our government's forthright acknowledgment of our goal, and an explanation of its importance. Under the limp banner of "détente," intimidated by media pejoratives against "cold war rhetoric," recent American presidents and secretaries of state had learned to speak softly to the Russians and toast Chairman Mao in Peking, ignoring the anti-human nature of the despotic Communist regimes.

President Carter's earnest and sincere initiatives on human rights, despite his administration's frequent bumbling and sometimes gutless backtracking, have to some degree changed that.

"Human rights," like all good political phrases, is a code-phrase. It means far more than attempting to secure the rights of dissent for a relative handful of brave activists in the Communist states. What it connotes is immeasurably broader: that the U.S. understands again, publicly and unashamedly, that it stands for a profound moral ideology, that that ideology is under attack, and that we must rally ourselves and our like-minded allies to defend it. One way of defending it, to be sure, is rhetorically. The power of words is very important.

But words alone aren't enough.

With our goal understood and our adversaries identified we must, if we're serious, use the tools that we possess; use them intelligently, cautiously, moderately, but by God, use them. Some of our best and most effective tools are economic.

Many in Washington recognize this fact. Accordingly, Congress is engulfed with proposed legislation, some wise, some not-so-wise, designed to use American wealth to give carrots to those nations which honor human rights and sticks to those that don't; legislation offering carrots to nations, free nations, that understand the problem and no carrots to those who don't or won't. In the Executive Branch, bureaucrats are devising methods to thwart both over-eager Congressmen on the one hand, and repressive Communists on the other.

Now, the tool of economic power is two-edged, complicated and sometimes mystifying. Some of its complications and mysteries were spelled out in the preceding pages. It is not the intention of this work to offer a detailed U.S. economic-political strategy. We suggest only that such a strategy should be devised and implemented, and that at this point in world history it can be pursued without bringing ruin to the MNCs, despair to free enterprise ideologues, or war to the rest of us.

Our only problem with our composite Activist's view of the wealth weapon is that, despite disclaimers, he is perhaps too active an Activist. Those interested in wealth weaponry must remember always how porcupines make love—very, very, carefully. The weapon is a scalpel, not a meat clever.

One tactical note: As potential scalpel-wielders, we suggest that it is obviously more important to use economic leverage on the Soviet Union and Eastern Europe, than against Chile and South Korea. The government in Santiago does not control missiles pointed at Chevy Chase, nor does it attempt to change the political nature of other countries. Moreover, it is open to the force of our moral example and our censure as Moscow is not, at least not now.

So where does this leave us? Consider the political and strategic use of American economic power from this perspective: A third of a century after World War II, a new era of big power relationships, marked by greater approximate equality, has clearly begun. The U.S., some say, is no longer the undisputed dominant power, and the limits of our military strength, our political influence and our financial capability are plainly in sight. Democracy, once a seemingly universal ideal, is now a challenged force in the world.

Some wise men are no longer wholly sure that this is the American Century, after all. And yet . . . America is not just another country and cannot be as long as people within and outside our borders believe in the promise made at the birth of this idealized country. This was the truth at the core of President Carter's early campaign for human rights. One who believes is the Russian émigré writer, Andrei Amalrik, who in 1976 received the annual award of the International League for Human Rights. In his speech after receiving the award, he spoke directly to the American people:

> And now, in appealing to you, I am appealing to the American revolutionary spirit. I appeal to your desire to sow the seeds of a new revolution, not to your desire to live undisturbed, paying for your tranquility with credits, wheat and Pepsi-Cola. I appeal to the spirit of Jefferson and not the spirit of Kissinger!
>
> I am a better realist than the exponents of so-called *realpolitik*. You shall never feel safe while you compromise with violence instead of fighting against it. The battle has been thrust upon you and you will not succeed in dodging it."

It is in the spirit of Jefferson (a spirit that Kissinger evermore frequently invokes these days) that the authors see the issues raised. It is in the spirit of Jefferson that we believe our composite characters and the forces they represent can resolve the issues raised here. We seek, not the false perpetuation of an idealized and mythical U.S., but the swift re-emergence of an intelligent, self-aware, and muscular U.S. to make its revolutionary way in the real world. In this enterprise, all else, including business, is a secondary matter.

Index

"Acme Widget Factory," 40, 47–48, 85, 88, 97
Adelman, M.A., 59
Afghanistan, 55, 66, 119
AFL–CIO, 3
Agri-power, 66–67, 74
Airplanes, 7
Algeria, 79
Allende, Salvatore y Gossens, 11
Amalrik, Andre, 122
American Establishment, 33
"American way of life," 54–56
Anaconda Steel, 41
Andean Pact, 29
Angola, 64, 67, 119
Anti-Americanism, 109–110
Anti-multinational corporation bias, 22
Arabs, 9, 13, 90
Argentina, 31
Ashland Oil, 11
Australian multinational corporations, 26, 54
Automation, 45
Auto Sales, 49

Baja California: copper in, 27
Balance of payments, 37
Ball, George, 97
Banking multinationals, 29–39
Bauxite, 10, 23
Beef, 73
Belgium, 100
Bicycles, 34
Big Business–Left-Wing coalition, 66
Blue jeans, 35
Blumenthal, Michael, 66
Bolivia, 29, 95
Bougainville Copper Ltd., 26
Brady, Laurence J., 12
Brazil, 3, 31–32, 43, 56, 95; auto radios in, 120
Brezhnev, Leonid, 48
Bribery, 105, 112
"Businessgate," 32

Cameras, 7
Camper trailers, 39
Canada, 23, 43

Capitalism, 7, 10, 20, 43–44, 55–56, 64, 76, 78 105
Cartels, 10; cartel-breaking mechanisms, 74
Carter, Jimmy, 54, 68–69, 120–21; administration of, 2, 51, 66–67, 97; and human rights, 54
Cattle-breeding program, 32
Center for International Affairs (Harvard University), 75
Champion International, 31
Chase Manhattan Bank, 26
Chicken raising, 32
Chile, 11, 15, 29, 33, 41, 68–69, 121
China, 3, 62, 90, 118
CIA, 11, 119
Citicorp, 33
"Club of Rome," 80
Clothing manufacturers, 6
Coal, 103
Cocoa, 10
Coffee, 10
Cold War, 58
Colombia, 29
Commerce Department, 12, 66
Comparative advantage, 7–8, 25, 49, 102
Computers, 7, 22, 25, 45
Continental Group, 37–38
Copper, 5, 10, 23, 26–27, 48, 56
Cortisone, 45
Cubans, 55, 119

D-marks, 14
Danielian, N.R., 19
Decline of the West, 55
Defense Department, 45
Defense Intelligence Agency, 12
Détente, 11–16, 58, 65–66, 91–92
Democratic party, 3, 58, 66
Djilas, Milovan, 61
Dollar, 14, 28, 42–44
Double-digit inflation, 14
Dress manufacturers, 5
Drouin, Pierre, 30
Drugs, 45, 87
Dulles, John Foster, 66
Duncan, Sir Val, 29
DuPont de Nemours and Co, E. I., 18

Economic jingoism, 56; policy-maker, 33
Ecuador, 29, 60
Electric typewriters, 24
Electronics, 49
England, 3, 17, 26, 35–36, 43, 46, 54, 61, 96, 104
"Eurodollar," 30
Export-import bank credits, 63
Exports, 72–73
Extractive multinational corporations, 25–29; functions of (oil, mining), 22
Extractive wealth, 22, 25
Exxon, 9

F-4 Phantom, 49
Federal Reserve Board, 30
Firestone Tire and Rubber Company, 32
Foreign policy, 53–75, 103
Foreign tax payments, 50. See also taxes
Ford, Gerald R., 63–64; administration of, 66–67
Ford Motor Company, 31
Fortune-500 Corporations, 48
Fourth World, 104
France, 42–43, 96, 100, 104
Francs, 14
Free enterprise system, 39–40

General Agreement on Trade and Tariff (GATT), 51–52, 73, 84
General Electric, 40, 43
Germany, 3, 7, 23–25, 35, 42, 96, 104; corporations in, 87, 99
Gilpin, Robert, 43–44, 50
Global Reach, 23
GNP, 34, 48, 57, 79
Grain sales, 7, 64
Great Britain. See England
Greece, 55
Gulf Oil Corp., 11, 33

Haq, ul Mahhub, 78–79
Hatfield, Robert S., 38
Helsinki Agreement, 61
High-technology function of multinational corporations (jet aircraft, computers), 22

Hoffer, Eric, 109–10
Holland, 11, 17, 96, 100
Hong Kong, 3, 6
Hostage-taking, 51
Hughes Tool Company, 11
Human rights, 54, 61–62, 69, 91, 120, 122
Huntington, Samuel, 2, 66
Hydrocarbons, 13
Hydropower, 26

IBM, 12–13, 24, 25, 110
Imported passenger cars, 6–7
India, 105
Indochina, 119
International Banking Consortium, 26
International Brotherhood of Electrical Workers, 43
International Economic Policy Association, 19
International Management and Development Institute, 31
Iran, 3, 11, 15, 51, 55, 66, 77, 80
Irishmen, 100
Iron Curtain countries, 12
Israel, 61
Italy, 7, 11, 32; city-states of, 17; shoe-industry in, 7, 95
ITT, 11, 33, 111
Ivory Coast, 95

Jackson Amendment, 62–64, 66–68, 90, 95
Jackson, Henry, 2, 62
Japan, 3, 7–8, 11–13, 20, 24–25, 32, 35, 39, 54, 72, 96, 104; motorcycles in, 86, 95
Jet aircraft, 45, 49, 86
Job export, 14

Kama River Truck Plant, 12, 96
Karpel, Craig, 60
Kendall, Donald, 13
Kennecott Copper Corp., 27
"Kennedy Round," 84, 110
Keynes, Lord, 43
Khrushchev, Nikita, 110

Kissinger, Henry, 12, 27, 55, 58, 63–64, 66, 78, 91–92, 122
Kreps, Juanita, 2, 66

Labor-intensive functions of multinational corporations (shoes, textiles), 22, 24
Labor: leaders, 57, 91, 93; movement, 40–52, 99; unions, 34
Lasers, 45
Le Monde, 30
Lenin, 13, 110
Lesotho, 48
Less-developed countries (LDCs), 25–26, 28, 103
Levi Strauss and Co., 35
Liberia, 32
Lincoln, Abraham, 110
Lipset, Seymour Martin, 110
Lockheed Corp., 11, 32
Low Countries: city-states in, 17. See Belgium and Holland
Low-technology functions of multinational corporations (autos, consumer electronics), 22, 24

Machine tool plants, 8
Malaya, 100; Malaysia, 110, 120
Manufacturing multinationals, 23–25
Marshall Plan, 7, 38
McCloy, John J., 33
McDonnell Douglas, 49
Mexico, 27, 31, 120
Mexico City, 21
Michelin, 87
Middle East, 11, 55, 104
MIGs, 66
Mineral wealth, 10, 26, 78, 81, 103
Ministry of International Trade and Industry (MITI), 72
Minnesota Mining and Manufacturing Company, 11
Mitsubishi, 49
"Most Favored Nation" (MFN), 62, 71, 95
Motorboats, 39
Movies, 10
Moynihan, Daniel F., 66, 68

Multinational corporations (MNCs), 1, 5–6, 8, 10, 13–17, 20, 27–29, 32, 34, 36, 41, 56, 70–71, 82, 84, 90, 101, 105, 112, 118

National Institutes of Health, 45
Natural gas, 103
Nestlè's, 87
New Deal, 78, 103
New Guinea, 26–27, 41
New International Economic Order, 10–11, 14, 82, 92, 117–18
New Zealand, 89, 95
Nigeria, 42, 60
Nixon, Richard M., 11–12, 50, 58, 91; administration of, 66–67; leader of proto-totalitarians, 116
Nyerere, Julius, 77

Office of Export Administration, 12
Oil, 9, 14, 23, 29, 42, 56, 59, 81; embargo on, 51
"One World," 17–19
OPEC, 9, 11, 14, 28, 30, 50, 58–61, 67, 77–78, 81, 92, 94, 100, 118–19
Orderly Market Agreement (OMA), 113–14
Organization for Economic Cooperation and Development (OECD), 34, 57, 97
Overseas corporate bribery, 32
Overseas Private Investment Corporation (OPIC), 75

Pakistan, 78
Pepsico, 13
Perez, Andres, 78
Peru, 29, 31, 90, 95
Petro-dollars, 29
"Petroleum Buying Board," 59
Pfizer, Inc., 37
Phillipines, 35
Phillips Petroleum, 87
Phoenicians, 17
Phonographs, 49
Pinochet government, 68
Point Four, 7, 38
Poland, 100
Poverty, 10, 93

Project Independence, 50
Protectionism, 34
Proto-totalitarianism, 116; See Nixon, Richard M.
Pulp and paper industry, 31

Radar, 86
Radios, 10, 34, 49; transistors, 6
Recession, 14
Republican ideology, 3, 55, 58, 66
Rhodes, Cecil, 100
Rhodesia, 90
Rockefeller, David, 26, 33
Roosevelt, Franklin D., 99
Rubber, 32
Rusk, Dean, 53
Russia. See U.S.S.R.

Sakharov, Andrei, 64
SALT, 66
Samuelson, Paul, 21–22
Sanyo, 24
Saudi Arabia, 50, 65
Scharansky trials, 61
Schumpeter, Joseph, 89
Scotland, 6
Securities and Exchange Commission, 11
Sears Roebuck, 110
Semiconductor Industry Association, 73
Semiconductors, 45, 72–73
Service functions of multinational corporations (banking and finance), 22
Sewing machines, 5, 49
Shapiro, Irving S., 18
Sheet Metal Workers Union, 41
Shell Oil Company, 87
Shoe manufacturing, 7–8, 34, 49
Siberia: natural pipeline in, 13
Sicilian peasants, 100
Simon, William, 68
Singer Sewing Machine Company, 6
Smith, Adam, 7, 25, 49, 114
Solzhenitsyn, Aleksandr, 13
Sony, 24, 87
South Africa, 105
Southeast Asia, 11, 55

South Korea, 33, 118, 120
Soviet Union. *See* U.S.S.R.
Spain, 17
Spengler, Oswald, 55
Stagflation, 47, 59
State Department, 31, 68, 89
Steel, 49, 73
Steroids, 45
Stevenson, Adlai, 63
Subcommittee on Multinational Corporations, U. S. Senate, 11
Sugar, 101
Sweden, 61, 96
Switzerland, 3, 96

Taipei, 48
Taiwan, 3, 9, 35, 42, 47, 118, 120
Tanzania, 77
Tape recorders, 49
Taxes, 87, 112; tax code, 70; tax credits, 50; tax deductions, 50; tax deferral, elimination of, 50, 70; selective reinstatement of, 70. *See also* foreign tax payments
Technical design licenses, 28
Teflon, 45
"Ten Ways to Break OPEC," 60
Tetracycline, 45
Textiles, 73, 101
Thailand, 35
Third World, 6, 10, 27, 58, 61, 65–68, 71, 76–82, 99, 104, 117–19
Tin, 10, 23, 95
Tokyo, 21, 84
Toynbee, Arnold, 18
Trademark licenses, 28
Transistors, 6. *See also* radios
Trilateral Commission, 67
Turkey, 54–55
"Turn-key" factory, 46

TVs, 6, 10, 24, 39, 49, 74, 86. *See also* Whirlpool

Ukraine, 100
"Uncle Sugar," 1, 8, 41, 72, 113
United Fruit Company, 28
United Nations, 28, 68; Declaration of Human Rights, 62
U.S. Power and the Multi-National Corporation, 44
United States, 1, 3, 7, 9, 11, 13, 20, 36–38, 40–41, 44, 46, 49, 51, 56, 59, 65, 78, 94, 109–10
U.S.S.R., 2–3, 11, 13, 20, 48, 51, 61–63, 66, 68, 73, 89, 111, 117, 121

Vance, Cyrus, 64
Venezuela, 29, 78
Vernon, Richard, 75
Vietnam, 11, 58, 62, 119
Volkswagen, 24, 99
Voluntary quotas, 35, 113
Vorona, Jack, 12

Warsaw Pact, 13, 54
Washington, D. C., 21
Wealth of Nations, 7
Whirlpool: TV, 24. *See also* TVs
Willkie, Wendell, 17
Women's apparel, 49
World Bank, 28, 78
Wrigley chewing gum, 38
Wriston, Walter, 33

"Yankee cultural imperialism," 31, 51
Yen, 14
Yugoslav dissident, 61

Zaire, 41
Zinc, 29

World Trade 35, 48